THE GOSPEL
AND ITS MINISTRY

THE GOSPEL
AND ITS MINISTRY

by
Sir Robert Anderson

KREGEL PUBLICATIONS
Grand Rapids, Michigan 49501

THE GOSPEL AND ITS MINISTRY, Copyright © 1978
by Kregel Publications, a division of Kregel, Inc.
All rights reserved.

Library of Congress Cataloging in Publication Data

Anderson, Robert, Sir, 1841-1918.
  The Gospel and its Ministry.

  (Sir Robert Anderson library)
  Reprint of the 18th ed. published by
Pickering & Inglis, London.
  Includes index.
  1. Salvation. I. Title. II. Series:
Anderson, Robert, Sir, 1841-1918.
Sir Robert Anderson library.
BT751.A6   1978   234   78-9539
ISBN 0-8254-2126-8

Printed in the United States of America

CONTENTS

Publisher's Preface vi
Preface viii

1. Introduction 1
2. Grace 9
3. The Cross 24
4. Faith 38
5. Repentance and the Spirit's Work . . 56
6. Election 75
7. Substitution 87
8. Righteousness 101
9. Sanctification 117
10. Reconciliation 136
11. Justification by Faith 153
12. Justification by Works 159
13. Justification by Blood 163
14. Holiness and Sanctification 168
15. Cleansed by Blood 173
16. The Priesthood of Christ 179
17. Atonement 185
18. The Godhood of God 196

Appendices

1. Miracles 203
2. Texts where ἁγιάζω occurs 206
3. Texts where Caphar. occurs . . . 208
4. The Fatherhood of God 209
Index 211

PUBLISHER'S PREFACE

The latter part of the nineteenth century brought a new plague to the Christian world. It was called the "textual criticism movement." Using the so-called scholarly approach, men were alleging the Word of God to be filled with errors and mistakes. Each so-called mistake took another page from the Holy Writ of God, weakened the foundation for faith, and watered down the basic message of the Bible, the Gospel of the Lord Jesus Christ.

Into such a morass came the preaching of the faithful expositors of the Bible and the writings of such men as Sir Robert Anderson. In the face of such criticism, the introduction of *The Gospel and Its Ministry* brought peace to troubled minds as men and women recalled what the Gospel had brought into their lives. The textual criticism was met with Truth and its fruit . . . peace and joy.

The attempts of Satan to undermine the Word of God have not decreased, nor have the proponents of textual criticism ceased to expound their ideas. For this reason, if no other, the new edition of this book is timely and very necessary. People once again can see the purpose and plan of God for His revelation. Believers can have that peace and joy that comes with a solid foundation and full trust in the Gospel resultant in a faith which transforms the hearts and lives of men.

Robert Anderson maintains that the Gospel and its provisions for man are still the answer to the longing heart and the empty life. God has provided all that man needs for salvation and for the difficult journey through this life. Where will man find this peace with God and the peace of God? At the feet of the Lord Jesus and in the teachings of the Apostle Paul, who has recorded the Words of God that give meaning and purpose to the Christian life.

We lift our voices in thanks to Dr. Anderson who saw the problems of the coming generation and its rank unbelief. We issue the call to all believers everywhere to return to the study of the Book of Books and to believe that God has given us all we need in the Gospel and all the power we need to perform its ministry.

The Publishers

PREFACE

IN these days men have left off faith. The spirit of the martyrs is not in them. Opinions have taken the place of convictions ; and the result is a liberality which is the offspring, not of humility and love, but of indifference or doubt. Opinions are our own, and should not be too firmly held. Truth is Divine, and is worth living for and dying for.

But what is truth ? Each one, surely, must answer for himself ; and does it not resolve itself therefore into a question of *opinion* after all ? This is just what characterises the day we live in. Listening to the discordant voices that abound on every side, men are content to give heed only to the points on which the greater number appear to be agreed ; and even these are held on sufferance till some new voice is raised to challenge them. FAITH is impossible. If an angel from heaven were heard above the discord, or an apostle should return to earth, then indeed the anarchy of opinion might yield once again to the reign of faith. Meanwhile, we must be content to drift on in darkness, blindly trusting that when the day dawns we shall find ourselves in safety.

Was it for this the Son of God lived and died on earth ? Was it for this " the glorious Gospel of the blessed God " was preached " with the Holy Ghost sent down from heaven " ? How different from the spirit of the age is the language of the inspired Apostle ! " Though WE or an ANGEL FROM HEAVEN preach any other gospel unto you than that which we have preached unto you, let him be accursed." Such warnings in Holy Writ are not the words of wild exaggeration. In the last days the new light which men seek for to dispel " the deepening gloom " will not be wanting ; but it will prove a wrecker's fire, though seemingly accredited as the beacon light of truth.

God has given us a revelation. And, while doubt still lingers round innumerable questions on which we crave knowledge, Divine certainty is our privilege in respect of " all things that pertain unto life and godliness." The man who would force his opinions on others is a boor. He who would die for his opinions is a fool. But Christianity has not to do with *opinions*. It is founded on established facts and Divine truth ; and faith based thereon is the heritage of the Church. Her martyrs knew the power of faith. The truth they died for was not " the general sense of Scripture corrected in the light of reason and conscience," and thus reduced to the pulp-like consistency of modern theology. In the solitude of the dungeon, or amidst the agonies of the rack, they calmly rested on the Word of God ; and, even when assured that all others had recanted, they could stand firmly against both the world and the Church. Faith, which makes the unseen a present reality, brought all heaven into their hearts, and, refusing to accept deliverance, they braved death in every form.

We are not called upon to wear the martyr's crown, but it is ours to share the martyr's faith. We can have no toleration for the veiled scepticism which is passing for Christianity to-day. Agnosticism is Greek for ignorance, and ignorance is both shameful and sinful in presence of a Divine revelation. The Christian is not ignorant ; neither is he in doubt. We do not *think* this or that : we KNOW. " We know that the Son of God is come." " We know that He was manifested to take away our sins." " We know that we have passed from death unto life." " We know that if our earthly house were dissolved, we have a building of God, eternal in the heavens." " We know that when He shall appear we shall be like Him."

It is in this spirit that " The Gospel and Its Ministry " is written. The book is designed to confirm faith, not to suggest doubts. And what distinguishes it from many other valuable works on the same great subject, is that it is not hortatory but doctrinal in character. Addressed to no special class, it is intended for all who are interested in the *doctrine* of the Gospel.

1

INTRODUCTION

"God so loved the world, that he gave His only begotten Son, that whosoever believeth in Him should not perish, but have everlasting life."—JOHN iii. 16.

JUST as an infant's hand can grasp the acorn which holds " the giant oak " within it, so the youngest child who can lisp " the Nicodemus sermon " may with truth be said to know the gospel, and yet in every word of it there is a depth and mystery of meaning which God alone can fathom. Tell me what it means to *perish*, and enable me to grasp the thought of a life that is eternal. Measure for me the abyss of man's wickedness and guilt during all the ages of his black and hateful history, that I may realise in some degree what that world is which God has loved ; and then, pausing for a moment in wonder at the thought that such a world could be loved at all, hasten on to speak of love that gave the Son. And when you have enabled me to know this love, which cannot be known, for it passes knowledge, press on still and tell me of the sacrifice by which it has measured and proved itself—His Son, His Only-begotten Son. Make me to know, in the fulness of knowledge, Him who declared that the Father alone could know Him.[1] And when you have achieved all this, I turn again to the words of Christ, and I read that it was GOD who so loved the world, and I crave to know Who and What God is. I can rise to the thought of love, perhaps even to an evil world, and the conception of love giving up an only son is not beyond me ; but when I come to know that it was GOD who loved, that GOD was the giver, and GOD's Son the gift, I stand as a wondering worshipper in the presence of the Infinite, and confess that such knowledge is too high for me.

At the very threshold, therefore, I charge my reader to think becomingly of the gospel, remembering that it is the gospel of GOD. And His gospel is like Himself. The heaven of heavens cannot contain Him, and yet He owns the humble heart as a fitting home.[2] So also, in its simplicity and plainness, the good news is within the reach of the youngest and most ignorant, aye, and even of the lowest and the worst, for such may hear and believe and live ; but in its depth and fulness it is known to God alone, for it is a revelation of Himself. Hence it is that the old song of the redeemed on earth will be a new song throughout eternity ;[3] for every advance we make in the knowledge of

[1] Matt. xi. 27.　　[2] Isa. lvii. 15.　　[3] Rev. v. 9 ; xiv. 3.

God will shed new light on the message we received in our sins and sorrows here.

But not only has the gospel a depth and dignity and glory all its own because it is in a special sense a revelation of God, it has also a distinctive greatness and solemnity by virtue of its peculiar mission, and of the issues involved in the proclamation of it. It is divinely called " the power of God unto salvation to every one that believeth." [1] The power of God! no words can add force to this, and words that detract from it are impious. The mighty power which made the worlds and alone can raise the dead, such is its power to the sinner who believes. Let the preacher remember this ; and while he humbly consecrates to God every talent he possesses, let him never attempt by unworthy means to add attractiveness to such a message.

And what solemn issues are depending while it is being proclaimed! For the preaching of the gospel must ever tend to life, or else to death, in those who hear. How terrible then to be guilty of levity in such a ministry !

In the iron days of Rome, public triumphs were sometimes accorded to victorious generals in acknowledgment of brilliant services. Clad in gold and purple, his feet bedecked with pearls, and a golden crown upon his brow, the victor entered the city of the Empire in a chariot of ivory and gold. Triumphal music mingled with the rapturous shouts that greeted him, and the air was filled with the sweet perfume of flowers and spices scattered on

[1] Rom. i. 16..

his path. Waggons passed on before, filled with the spoils and trophies of his victories. The senate and the priesthood attended in his honour. In front of his chariot the doomed captives marched in chains, while behind him followed the company of those who had been set at liberty or ransomed. All Rome kept holiday, and joined with one accord to swell the triumph of the conqueror.

It is to such a scene that St. Paul alludes in his Second Epistle to the Corinthians when speaking of the gospel; for its ministry, whatever the results in those who hear, is Christ's triumph none the less. "Thanks be unto God, who always leadeth us in triumph in Christ, and maketh manifest through us the savour of His knowledge in every place."[1] We are a savour of life to the ransomed throng, and of death to the doomed and fettered captives. But whether our ministry swell the glad company of the redeemed, or add to the condemnation of those that perish, we are none the less, in the one as in the other, a sweet savour of Christ unto God.

Can any amount of education or of training make men "sufficient" for such a ministry as this? "Who," the apostle demands, "is sufficient for these things?" And the answer is not doubtful, "Our sufficiency is from God, who also made us sufficient as ministers of a new covenant."[2] And how? The halo that encircled Moses' face at Sinai betokened the glory of his ministry. But that ministry, glorious though it was, had no glory in comparison with the ministry now entrusted to

[1] 2 Cor. ii. 14–16, R.V.   [2] 2 Cor. iii. 5, 6, R.V.

men.[1] What then shall we expect in him whom God has made " sufficient " as a minister of the new covenant ? We turn to behold a poor creature, troubled on every side, perplexed and persecuted and cast down, in bodily presence weak, in speech contemptible, held in repute as so much filth and scum,[2] and in him we find the man whom God deemed fit for a ministry so glorious and so great. And the secret of his fitness was in this, that the knowledge of the glory of God lit up his heart, and was reflected back with a heavenlier light than that which dazzled Israel's gaze.[3]

Such was the great apostle, and such his fitness. And can any one suppose that mental training and moral culture can avail if this " sufficiency " be wanting ; or that if men lack both culture and training they are in a better case ! But this was not all. With natural advantages that were entirely exceptional,[4] and in spiritual attainments unsurpassed, pre-eminent among ministers of Christ in his labours and sufferings, and as to his office " not a whit behind the very chiefest apostles," for, in proof of his apostleship, he could appeal not only to his unexampled life, but to " signs and wonders and mighty deeds " which he had wrought ; yet, when " in the foolish confidence of boasting " he ransacked his history for a crowning proof of his

---

[1] 2 Cor. iii. 7–11. In Ex. xxxiv. 33, the A.V. suggests a false meaning, by inserting *till*, instead of *when*. Moses spoke to the people with unveiled face, but when he ceased speaking he put on a veil that they might not see the glory fading ; they were not to know that the glory of the old covenant was transitory.

[2] 2 Cor. iv. 8, 9 ; 1 Cor. iv. 13.

[3] 2 Cor. iv. 6.   [4] Acts xxii. 3 ; Phil. iii. 4–6.

" sufficiency " as a minister of Christ, he turned away from all these things to tell how, crushed doubtless, and sick at heart, he was once bundled out of Damascus in a basket to escape the Roman garrison that held the city to apprehend him.[1] Or if he goes on to tell of being caught up to the highest heaven, and of hearing there unspeakable words impossible for man to utter, he may glory indeed in such a Paul, for this was for him a brief foretaste of the day when the redeemed shall bear the image of the heavenly. But if he must boast of the servant and apostle here, he will point to the Damascus flight and the " thorn in the flesh," " Satan's messenger to buffet him." [2]

Would that every one who claims to preach the gospel, whether arrayed in silk and lawn, or clad in corduroy and frieze, would ponder this paradox of the ministry of Paul. Let us picture to ourselves this mighty apostle, this greater and more glorious than Moses, smuggled out through a window in a buck-basket ! and then let us search out the meaning of this mystery, that he appeals to this his shame as the crowning boast of his whole life's labours. The answer in words is not far to seek, but which of us has grasped its meaning ? " Most gladly will I rather glory in my infirmities, that the power of Christ may rest upon me   Therefore I take pleasure in infirmities, in reproaches, in necessities, in persecutions, in distresses, for Christ's sake ; for when I am weak, then am I strong." [3]

What God wants in those whom He will put in trust with the gospel, is not that they shall be

[1] 2 Cor. xi. 16–33   [2] 2 Cor. xii. 1–7.   [3] 2 Cor. xii. 9, 10.

polished and educated gentlemen, much less that they shall be coarse and ignorant boors ; not that they shall be skilled in dogmatic theology, much less that they shall be unlearned in doctrine ; not that they shall be brilliant and eloquent, much less that they shall be ungifted and dull. All He seeks is a fitting instrument upon whom the power of Christ can rest, an empty earthen vessel that He can fill with His priceless treasure. The man, whoever he may be, whether on the highest round of the social ladder, or the lowest, who can say with Paul, " Most gladly will I glory in infirmities, that the power of Christ may rest on me," and say it with unfeigned lips, and from a heart that has been taught it in the school of God, has gained the secret of this competency for the ministry of reconciliation.

Apart from this fitness, the highest and the greatest are but " clouds without water," while with it the lowest and the least may become " competent ministers of the new covenant." [1]

[1] The ministry of *the Gospel* is the special subject of these pages ; but the same fitness is essential to the ministry of the Church. The Apostle Paul was called to the double ministry (" The gospel, . . . whereof I Paul am made a minister ; . . . the church, whereof I am made a minister."—Col. i. 23–25). Both these ministries are, no doubt, included in the title, " ministers of God " (2 Cor. vi. 4), or " ministers of Christ " (2 Cor. xi. 23). The ministers are specially named, along with the elders or bishops, in the address of the Epistle to the Philippians (Phil. i. 1) ; and the characteristics which were to be sought for in any who claimed that position are specified in 1 Tim. iii. 8–13. The word *minister* is derived from the Latin ; *deacon* from the Greek. Etymologically, and in their origin, the words are synonyms. But *deacon* has in English acquired a meaning of its own ; and its retention in the Revised Version is a flagrant violation of the avowed principles on which the revision

was conducted. It is hard to believe, moreover, that it was not committed intentionally, to perpetuate the popular error of supposing that the deacon was a subordinate office-bearer in the Church. That it is an error is sufficiently clear from the fact that the Apostle Paul so describes himself seven times.

The word διάκονος occurs thirty times in the New Testament. In the Gospels it is used eight times, where it means a servant in the ordinary sense, save only in John xii. 26. The other places where it is used are the following passages in the Epistles of Paul :—Rom. xiii. 4 ; xv. 8 ; xvi. 1 ; 1 Cor. iii. 5 ; 2 Cor. iii. 6 ; vi. 4 ; xi. 15, 23 ; Gal. ii. 17 ; Eph. iii. 7 ; vi. 21 ; Phil. i. 1 ; Col. i. 7, 23, 25 ; iv. 7 ; 1 Thess. iii. 2 ; 1 Tim. iii. 8, 12 ; and iv. 6, where Timothy is called a " deacon." The word is never applied to Stephen and his fellows (Acts vi.), with whom it is popularly associated. Διακονία is used in Acts vi. 1 (ministration), and also in ver. 4 (ministry). It occurs thirty-four times in the New Testament ; once in its ordinary acceptation of " serving " (Luke x. 40), and generally as equivalent to " ministry " (e.g. 2 Tim. iv. 5, 11).

2

GRACE

" THE GOSPEL OF THE GLORY OF THE BLESSED GOD ! " [1]

" Show me Thy glory, I beseech Thee," was the prayer of Moses ; and God answered, " I will make all My goodness pass before thee, and I will proclaim the name of Jehovah before thee, and will be gracious to whom I will be gracious, and will show mercy on whom I will show mercy." [2] God's highest glory displays itself in sovereign grace, therefore it is that the gospel of His grace is the gospel of His glory.

Let us take heed then that we preach grace. He who preaches a mixed gospel robs God of His glory, and the sinner of his hope. They for whom these pages are intended, need not be told that salvation is only by the blood ; but many there are who preach the death of Christ, without ever rising to the truth of grace. " Dispensational truth," as it is commonly called, is deliberately rejected by not a few ; and yet without understanding the change which the death of Christ has made in God's relationships with men, grace cannot be apprehended.

[1] 1 Tim. i. 11 ; *not* " the glorious gospel."   [2] Ex. xxxiii. 18, 19.

It is not that God can ever change, or that the righteous ground of blessing can ever alter, but that the standard of man's responsibility depends on the measure and character of the revelation God has given of Himself. God's judgments are according to pure equity. They must have strange thoughts of Him who think it could be otherwise. In the Epistle to the Romans we have the great principle of His dealings with mankind. " He will render to every man according to his deeds ; to them who, by patient continuance in well-doing, seek for glory and honour and immortality, eternal life " ; but to the rest, indignation and wrath ; tribulation and anguish upon evil-doers, but upon well-doers, glory, honour, and peace ; and this for all without distinction, whether Jews or Gentiles, under law or without law ; for God is no respecter of persons.[1]

But is the standard of well-doing the same for all ? Shall the same fruit be looked for from the wild olive as from the cultured tree ; from the mountain side in its native barrenness, as from the vineyard on the fruitful hill ? Far from it. The first two chapters of the Epistle to the Romans are unmistakable in this respect. The Gentile will be judged according to the light of nature, and of conscience neglected and resisted ; the Jew, by the revelation God entrusted to him. Paul's sermon at Athens is no less clear as regards the condition of the heathen. As he said at Lystra,[2] they were not left without a witness, in that God did good, and gave rain and fruitful seasons, filling

[1] Rom. ii. 6-11 ; see also John v. 29.   [2] Acts xiv. 8-18.

their hearts with food and gladness. By such things, he declares again in another place,[1] God's eternal power and Godhead are clearly seen, so that they are without excuse. And so here,[2] God left the heathen to themselves, not that they should forget Him, but that they should seek Him, even though it were in utter darkness, so that they should need to grope for Him—" to feel after Him, and find Him." And, though there was ignorance of God, He could wink at the ignorance and give blessing notwithstanding, for " He is a rewarder of diligent seekers." [3] Moreover, this is still the case with all whom the witness of the Holy Ghost has not yet reached. If it be asked whether any have, in fact, been saved thus, I turn from the question, though I have no doubt as to the answer.[4] There is no profit in speculations about the fate of the heathen ; their judgment is with God. But there is profit and blessing untold in searching into His ways and thoughts toward men, that we may be brought in adoration to exclaim, " O the depth of the riches both of the wisdom and knowledge of God ! "

But to resume : " The times of this ignorance God winked at ; but now commandeth all men everywhere to repent, because He hath appointed a day in the which He will judge the world in righteousness." [5] And the change depends on this, that God has now revealed Himself in Christ, and therefore ignorance of Him is a sin that shuts men up to judgment. See the Lord's sad utterance in John xv. 24, as a kindred truth. Indeed, the

---

[1] Rom. i. 20.   [2] Acts xvii. 22–31.   [3] Heb. xi. 6.
[4] See Acts x. 34, 35.   [5] Acts xvii. 30, 31.

whole Gospel of John is a commentary on it. Darkness had reigned, but God did not hold men accountable for darkness ; it was their misfortune, not their fault. But He did hold them accountable to value and obey the little light they had, " the candle set up within them," and the stars above their head—those gleams of heavenly light, which, though they failed to illumine the way, might at least suffice to direct their course. But now, a new era dawned upon the world , " The Word was made flesh and dwelt among us." [1] The Light had entered in ; the darkness was past, the true Light was shining. To turn now to conscience or to law was like men who, with the sun in the zenith, nurse their scanty rushlight, with shutters barred and curtains drawn ; like men who cast their anchor because the daylight has eclipsed the stars. The principle of God's dealings was the same, but the measure of man's conduct was entirely changed. It was no longer a question of conscience or of law, but of the Only-begotten in their midst.

It was in words of solemn, earnest truth that the blessed Lord replied to the inquiry, " What shall we do that we might work the works of God ? " " *This* (said He) is the work of God, that ye believe on Him whom He hath sent." [2] The question was a right one, and the answer enforced the unchanging principle, that the light they had was the measure of their responsibility. The same great truth is no less plainly stated in the Nicodemus sermon. This was the condemnation, not that men's deeds were evil, though for these too there shall be wrath

[1] John i. 14.　　　　　　　[2] John vi. 28, 29.

in the day of wrath, but that, because their deeds were evil, they had brought upon themselves a still direr doom ; light had come into the world, but they had turned from it and *loved* the darkness.[1]

But this is not all ; even yet the reign of grace had not begun. Grace was there truly, for " grace came by Jesus Christ " ; but, like Himself, it was in humiliation ; it had yet to be enthroned. Grace was there. No adverse principle came in to influence His ways and words ; but though pure and unmixed, as it must ever be, it was restrained. He had a baptism to be baptized with, and how was He straitened till it was accomplished ! While there was a single claim outstanding, a single tie unbroken, grace was hindered, though it could not be alloyed.

But now was about to come the world's great crisis—the most stupendous event in the history of man, the only event in the history of God ! He had laid aside His glory, and come down into the scene. At His own door [2] He had stood and knocked, but only to find it shut in His face. Turning thence, He had wandered an outcast into the world which His power had made, but He wandered there unknown. " His own received Him not " ; " the world knew Him not." As He had laid aside His glory, He now restrained His power, and yielded Himself to their guilty will. In return for pity He earned but scorn. Sowing kindnesses and

[1] John iii. 19.
[2] John i. 11. εἰς τὰ ἴδια ἦλθε can scarcely be expressed in English. The French idiom is more apt : " Il est venu chez soi, et les siens ne l'ont point reçu."

benefits with a lavish hand He reaped but cruelty and outrage. Manifesting grace He was given up to impious law without show of mercy or pretence of justice. Unfolding the boundless love of the mighty heart of God He gained no response but bitterest hate from the hearts of men.

THE SON OF GOD HAS DIED AT THE HANDS OF MEN! This astounding fact is the moral centre of all things. A bygone eternity knew no other future,[1] an eternity to come shall know no other past. That death was this world's crisis.[2] For long ages, despite conscience outraged, the light of nature quenched, law broken, promises despised, and prophets cast out and slain, the world had been on terms with God. But now a mighty change ensued. Once for all the world had taken sides. In the midst stood that cross in its lonely majesty. God on one side, with averted face; on the other, Satan, exulting in his triumph. The world took sides with Satan: His darling was in the power of the dog,[3] and there was none to help, none to pity.

There, we see every claim which the creature had on God for ever forfeited, every tie for ever broken. Promises there had been, and covenants; but Christ was to be the fulfiller of them all. If a single blessing now descend on the ancient people of His choice, it must come to them in grace.[4] Life,

[1] 1 Pet. i. 20; Rev. xiii. 8.

[2] Νῦν κρίσις ἐστὶ τοῦ κόσμου τούτου. John xii. 31.

[3] Ps. xxii. 20.

[4] Rom. xi. leaves no room to question whether Israel will in fact be blessed hereafter; but even their national blessings they will owe to grace.

and breath, and fruitful seasons freely given, had testified of the great Giver's hand, and declared His goodness ; but if " seedtime, and harvest, and the changing year, come on in sweet succession " still, in a world blood-stained by the murder of the Son, it is no longer now to creation claims we owe it, nor yet to Noah's covenant,[1] but wholly to the grace of God in Christ.

In proof of this I might cite prophecies and parables, and appeal to the great principles of God that are the basis of gospel doctrine, as above both parable and prophecy. Nay, I might leave it to men themselves, as Christ did, to decide between themselves and God.[2] But I rather turn again to that solemn utterance of the Lord, in view of His lifting up upon the tree : " Now is the judgment of this world."

" These things the angels desire to look into." [3] And if angels were our judges, what would be our doom ! For ages they had both witnessed and ministered the goodness of God to men. But yesterday the heavens had rung with their songs of praise, as they heralded the Saviour's birth in Bethlehem : " Peace on earth, goodwill to men." Goodwill ! and this was what had come of it ! Peace ! and this was what men turned it to ! What thoughts were theirs as, terror-struck, they beheld that scene on Calvary ! Crucified amid heartless jeers, and cruel taunts, and shouts of mingled hate and triumph ! Buried in silence and by stealth ; buried in sorrow, but in silence. He who hears in secret, heard the stifled cry from the broken hearts of Mary and the

[1] Gen. ix. 11-17.　　　[2] Matt. xxi. 40.　　　[3] 1 Pet. i. 12.

rest, and the smothered sobs that tore the breasts
of strong men bowed with grief—the last sad tribute
of love from the little flock now scattered. But
as for the world, no man's lamentation, no woman's
wail was heard ! They had cried, " Away with
Him, away with Him ! " and now they had made
good their cry : the world was rid of Him, and that
was all they wanted.

Angels were witnesses to these things. They
pondered the awful mystery of those hours when
death held fast the Prince of Life. The forty days
wherein He lingered in the scenes of His rejection
and His death—was it not to make provision for
the little company that owned His name, to gather
them into some ark of refuge from the judgment-fire,
so soon to engulph this ruined world ? And now,
the gates lift up their heads, the everlasting doors
are lifted up, and with all the majesty of God
the King of Glory enters in.[1] The Crucified of
Calvary has come to fill the vacant throne, the
Nazarene has been proclaimed the Lord of Hosts !

But, mystery on mystery ! the greatest mystery
of all is now—the mystery of grace. That throne
is vacant still. Those gates and doors that lifted
up their heads for Him are standing open wide.
Judgment waits. The sea of fire which one day
shall close in upon this world to wipe out its memory
for ever, is tided back by the word of Him who sits
upon the Father's throne in grace. When the Son
of Man returns for judgment, " *then* shall He sit
upon *His* glorious throne." [2] And how unutterably
terrible will be that judgment ! Half measures

[1] Ps. xxiv. 7–10.   [2] Matt. xxv. 31 ; comp. Rev. iii. 21.

are impossible in view of the cross of Christ. The day is past when God could plead with men about their *sins*.[1] The controversy now is not about a broken law, but about a rejected Christ. If judgment, therefore, be the sinner's portion, it must be measured by God's estimate of the murder of His Son ; a cup of vengeance, brimful, unmixed, from the treading of the " winepress of the fierceness and wrath of Almighty God." [2]

But if grace be on the throne, what limits can be set to it ? If that sin committed upon Calvary has not shut the door of mercy, all other sins together shall not avail to close it. If God can bless in spite of the death of Christ, who may not be blest ? Innocence lost, conscience disobeyed and stifled, covenants and promises despised and forfeited, law trampled under foot, prophets persecuted,

[1] For the believer, the question of sin was settled at the cross ; for the unbeliever, it is postponed to the day of judgment. " Who His own self bare our sins on His own body on the tree " (1 Pet. ii. 24). " The Lord knoweth how to reserve the unjust unto the day of judgment to be punished " (2 Pet. ii. 9).

The distinction between judgment and punishment is important. The criminal is judged before he leaves the court-house for the prison, but his punishment has yet to come—it is a consequence of judgment, not a part of it. All unbelievers are precisely on a level as regards judgment. " He that believeth on Him is not judged [the word is κρινω], but he that believeth not is judged already, because he hath not believed in the name of the only begotten Son of God " (John iii. 18). Here the moral and the immoral, the religious and the profane, stand together, and share the same doom. But when judgment, in the sense of punishment, is in question, there can be no equality ; every sentence shall be apportioned to the guilt of each by the righteous and omniscient Judge. See Rev. xx. 13 ; Matt. xii. 36 ; Luke xii. 47, 48 ; Jude 15 ; and 2 Pet. ii. 9, already quoted.

[2] Rev. xix. 15.

and last and unutterably terrible, the Only-begotten slain. And yet there is mercy still ! What a gospel that would be !

But " the gospel of the glory of the blessed God " is something infinitely higher still. It is not that Calvary has failed to quench the love of God to men, but that it is the proof and measure of that love. Not that the death of Christ has failed to shut heaven against the sinner, but that heaven is open to the sinner by virtue of that death. The everlasting doors that lifted up their heads for Him are open for the guiltiest of men, and the blood by which the Lord of glory entered there is their title to approach. The way to heaven is as free as the way to hell. In hell there is an accuser, but in heaven there is no one to condemn. The only being in the universe of God who has a right to judge the sinner is now exalted to be a Saviour.[1] Amid the wonders and terrors of that throne, He is a Saviour, and He is sitting there in grace.

The Saviour shall yet become the Judge , but judgment waits on grace. Sin has reigned, and death can boast its victories : shall grace not have its triumphs too ? As surely as the sin of man brought death, the grace of God shall bring eternal

[1] " The Father judgeth no man, but hath committed all judgment unto the Son " " I judge no man," the Lord says again in another place. " If any man hear My words and believe not, I judge him not ; for I came not to judge the world but to save the world " (John v. 22, viii. 15, xii. 47). The day of grace must end before the day of judgment can begin. " The acceptable year of the Lord " must run its course before the advent of " the day of vengeance." Compare Isa. lxi. 1, 2, with Luke iv. 16-21, and notice the precise point at which the Lord " closed the book."

life to every sinner who believes. *One* sin brought death, but grace masters *all* sin. If sin abounded, grace abounds far more. Grace is conqueror. GRACE REIGNS. Not at the expense of righteousness, but in virtue of it. Not that righteousness requires the sinner's death, and yet grace has intervened to give him life. Righteousness itself has set grace upon the throne in order that the sinner may have life : " That as sin hath reigned unto death, even so might grace reign, through righteousness, unto eternal life, through Jesus Christ our Lord." [1] Such is the triumph of the cross. It has made it possible for God to bless us in perfect harmony with everything He is, and everything He has ever declared Himself to be , and in spite of all that we are, and of all that He has ever said we ought to be.

I have already referred to Paul's allusion to the ancient military triumphs, when writing to the Corinthians. [2] The word there used occurs again in his Epistle to the Colossians : [3] " Having spoiled principalities and powers, He made a show of them openly, leading them in triumph in Him." In the hour of His weakness, our enemies became His own, and fastened upon Him to drag Him down to death ; but, leading captivity captive, He chained them to the chariot-wheels of His triumph, and made a public show of them. Just as Israel stood on the wilderness side of the sea, and saw Pharaoh and his hosts in death upon the shore, it is ours to gaze upon the triumphs of the cross. God there

[1] Rom. v. 21. I have thus sought to epitomise the argument of the passage, beginning at verse 12.

[2] See p. 3 *ante*. [3] Col. ii. 15.

has mastered sin, abolished death, and destroyed him who had the power of death.

God has become our Saviour. Our trust is not in His mercy, but in Himself. Not in divine attributes, but in the living God. " GOD is for us " ; the Father is for us ; the Son is for us ; the Holy Ghost is for us. It is God who justifies ; it is Christ that died ; and the Holy Ghost has come down to be a witness to us of the work of Christ, and of the place that work has given us as sons in the Father's house.

" Behold, God is my salvation ; I will trust and not be afraid : for the Lord JEHOVAH is my strength and my song ; He also is become my salvation."

THE NIGHT OF THE BETRAYAL

Hell has gone forth in power.
   And ye should wake and weep :
Could ye not watch one little hour !
   This night is not for sleep.

Earth trembles in the scale,
   Yet knows not of the fight,
And if her fearful foe prevail,
   It will be always night.

Unpitying as the grave,
   Fierce as the winter breeze,
And mightier than the mountain wave
   That sweeps o'er midnight seas,

The Prince of Darkness came :
   Woe to the hated race !
What man can meet that brow of flame,
   Or live before his face !

No seraph's sword of light,
   Reddened in righteous wrath,
Flashed downward from the crystal height
   To bar his onward path.

No trumpet's warning cry
 Rose through the silent air,
No battle shout went forth on high
 From guarding squadrons there.

Above, the holy light
 Slept on the mountain's breast ;
Beneath, the tender breath of night
 Hushed moaning woods to rest.

Yet ne'er shall blackest night
 Such deepened horror know,
While stars look down on Olives height,
 Or Kedron's waters flow.

For who shall tell His woes,
 Whose grief out-gloomed the night,
When His strong love, bright star ! arose,
 O'erfilling heaven with light ?

The gentlest heart on earth
 Must taste her sharpest woe ,
The tender plant of heavenly birth
 Hell's fiercest blast must know.

King ! of the wounded breast,
 King ! of the uncrowned brow,
What faithful heart shall bring Thee rest !
 What arm shall aid Thee now !

Lo, sheathed in shining light,
 Heaven's wondering warriors stand,
With pinions closed for downward flight,
 Waiting their Lord's command.

But never comes that word,
 That night knows yet no dawn,
And still must each impatient sword .
 Sleep on each thigh, undrawn.

Not Angels' deathless feet
 May dare the darkening path,
Arched by the thunder clouds that meet,
 Heavy with coming wrath.

Alone His steadfast eye
　Can cleave the rolling gloom,
Where that dread sentence flames on high,
　The sinner's death of doom.

Oh ! all ye Stars of light
　Veil all your glowing spheres ;
Weep out your radiance ; drown the night
　In dew of heaven's tears.

Poor Earth ! Go mourn beneath
　Thy withered roses now ;
Thy thorns alone may twine the wreath
　To crown the Victor's brow.

Firmer than Carmel's might,
　When the long-leaping tide
Shivers its thousand shafts of light
　Far up his patient side,

His will unshaken stands
　Though that wild sea of wrath,
Upsurging to its outmost bands,
　Breaks foaming on His path.

Soft breezes of the West
　That, sighing as ye go,
Bear ever on, with kindly breast,
　Each whispered human woe,

Here droop your wings and die
　Low murmuring at His feet,
Then rise and bear His victor cry
　Up the long golden street !

High Heralds of His birth,[1]
　Make His new honours known !
Tell how the Blood, despised on earth,
　Sparkles before the throne !

Lo ! struck from Star to Star,
　The gracious echoes fall
To this poor world that rolls afar,
　Lowest and last of all ;

---

[1] Luke ii. 13.

Soft, as from weeping skies
  Drops the sweet summer rain,
Yet clear through all earth's Babel cries-
  Hear them ye sons of men ;

Nor thrust His mercy back,
  Who claims your hearts to-day :
Oh ! kiss His feet. Their wounded track
  Hath crimsoned all the way.

3

THE CROSS

" THE preaching of the cross." It is on this the great truth of grace depends. Not the *death* of Christ merely, but "the cross." Synonyms are few in Scripture, and a change of words is not to please fastidious ears but to express a different or fuller thought. " The preaching of the cross is foolishness to them that perish." [1] Not so the preaching of the death of Christ, apart from the truths which cluster round "the cross." The whole fabric of apostate Christianity is based upon the fact of that death, and by virtue of it the Scarlet Woman shall yet sit enthroned as mistress of the world. The Saviour's death is owned as part of the world's philosophy. It is a fact and a doctrine which human wisdom has adopted, and rejoices in as the highest tribute to human worth. How great and wonderful must that creature be on whose behalf God has made so marvellous a sacrifice ! And thus God is made to pander to man's pride and sense of self-importance.

And as with the world's philosophy, so also is it with the world's religion. The doctrine of the *death* of Christ, if separated from " the cross,"

[1] 1 Cor. i. 18.

leaves human nature still a standing ground. It is consistent with creature claims and class privileges. Sinners of the better sort can accept it, and be raised morally and intellectually by it. But the preaching of the cross is " the axe laid to the root of the tree," the death-blow to human nature on every ground and in every guise. It is not merely that Christ has died—the great fact on which redemption depends ; but that that death has been brought about in a way and by means which manifest and prove not only the boundless and causeless love of God to man, but also the wanton and relentless enmity of man to God ; that that death, while it has made it possible for God, *in grace*, to save the guiltiest and worst of Adam's race, has made it impossible, even with God, that the worthiest and best could be saved except in grace. It has measured out the moral distance between God and man, and has left them as far asunder as the throne of heaven and the gate of hell. If God will now give blessing, He must turn back upon Himself, and find in His own heart the motive, just as He finds the righteous ground of it in the work of Christ. There is no salvation now for " the circumcision " as such—for diligent users of the means of grace, for earnest seekers, for anxious inquirers, for a privileged class under any name or guise. If such were granted special favour, " then were the offence of the cross ceased," [1] and grace would be dethroned.

Circumcision did not deny the death of Christ. On the contrary, it betokened covenants and class privileges granted by virtue of the great sacrifice

[1] Gal. v. 11, and see p. 30 *post.*

to which every ordinance in the old religion pointed.
But it utterly denied *the cross*, and grace as connected with the cross ; for there every covenant
was forfeited, every privilege lost. Before the
cross, therefore, circumcision was the outward sign
of covenant blessing ; but after the cross, it became
the token of apostasy. The cross has shut man
up to grace or judgment. It has broken down all
" partition walls," and left a world of naked sinners
trembling on the brink of hell. Every effort to
recover themselves is but a denial of their doom,
and a denial too of the grace of God, which stoops
to bring them blessing where they are and as they
are. The cross of Christ is the test and touch-stone
of all things. Man's philosophy, man's power,
man's religion—behold their work, the Christ of
God upon a gallows ! [1]

In distinguishing thus between the death of
Christ and " the cross," let me not be misunder-
stood. It is not that God ever separates them
thus. On the contrary, " the preaching of the cross "
is the emphasising and enforcing of the very facts
and truths which the heart of man always struggles
to divorce from the doctrine of redemption, but
which God has inseparably connected with it. The
idea of redemption was perfectly familiar to the
Jew, and every student knows how entirely it
accords with human philosophy. The Jew and
the Greek could shake hands upon it, and set out
together to seek the realisation of it. But the one
demanded signs of Messiahship, and the passion

[1] Religion, power, philosophy : Jerusalem, Rome, Athens : the
Jew, the Roman, and the Greek.

of the other was wisdom.[1] The death and resurrection of the Son of God, if accomplished in a manner which men would deem worthy of the Son of God, might have satisfied the one, as it did in fact, as soon as the cross was lost sight of, satisfy and charm the other. But the cross was a stumbling-block to the religious man, and folly to the wisdom-lover.[2] If human philosophy to-day adopts and glories in redemption, as in fact it does, it is just because the cross is forgotten ; and if, in spite of what Christianity is in the world and to the world, the Jew is still unchristianised, it is just because with him that cross can never be forgotten.

It is not, I repeat, that God ever separates them, but that man always does. A gospel that points to the death of Christ in proof of God's high estimate of man, and then turns the doctrine of that death into a syllogism, so that men, in no way losing self-respect, can calmly reason out their right to blessing by it, will give no offence to any one, nor be branded as foolishness. Such a gospel pays due deference to human nature, and satisfies man's sense of need without hurting in the least his pride. Such a gospel has, in fact, produced that marvellous anomaly, a Christian world. Even in Paul's day " the many " [3] were but hucksters of the Word of God. Their aim was to make their wares acceptable, to secure a trade, as it were, and so they sought popularity and an apparent success by corrupting the gospel to make it attractive to their hearers.[4] " As of sincerity, as of God, in the sight

[1] I Cor. i. 22.   [2] I Cor. i. 23.   [3] οἱ πολλοί, 2 Cor. ii. 17.
[4] Such is the meaning of the passage. The word used means,

of God," says the apostle in contrast with all this, " we speak in Christ." The gospel he preached would have created a Church in the midst of a hostile world. The gospel of " the many " has constituted the world itself the Church. And the fable of the wolf in sheep's clothing finds a strange fulfilment here, though indeed the metamorphosis is so complete that we are at a loss to distinguish either wolf or sheep remaining.

Rationalism and Ritualism are the great enemies of the cross. The First Epistle to the Corinthians touches on the one : the Epistle to the Galatians deals with the other. A gospel which pays court either to man's reason or man's religion will never fail to be popular. Well versed, no doubt, in Greek philosophy, and no careless student of human nature, Paul might have drawn all Corinth after him had he gone there " with excellency of speech or of wisdom " in announcing the testimony of God. He did " speak wisdom among the perfect," as witness his letter to the Romans, or indeed his letter to the Corinthians themselves. His argument for the resurrection, the germ and pattern of Bishop Butler's great masterpiece of reasoning,[1]

first, " to retail," and then, to resort to the malpractices common with hucksters, to adulterate or corrupt.

[1] " The design, then, of the following treatise will be to show . . . that the particular parts principally objected against in this whole dispensation, are analogous to what is experienced in the constitution and course of nature or providence ; that the chief objections themselves, which are alleged against the former, are no other than what may be alleged with like justness against the latter ; where they are found in fact to be inconclusive," etc.— *The Analogy* (Introduction).

This is precisely the argument of 1 Cor. xv. 36-44. The

would have charmed and won not a few of the disciples of Plato and the other brilliant men who raised unenlightened reason to its highest glory at the very time when the voice of revelation was being hushed amid the sad echoes of Malachi's wail over the apostasy of Jehovah's people. But just because the Greeks were wisdom-worshippers, he turned from everything that would pander to their favourite passion, and became a fool among them, a man of one idea, who knew nothing " save Jesus Christ, *even Him crucified.*" The enthronement of Christ on high and the glories of His return, are inseparable from the Christian's faith, but in Corinth it was *the cross* the apostle preached, the cross in all its marvellous attractiveness for hearts enlightened from on high, in all its intolerable repulsiveness for unregenerate men.[1]

With the Galatians it was against the *religion* of the flesh he had to contend. He testified to them that if they were circumcised Christ should profit them nothing.[2] How was this ? Had grace found its limits here, so that if any transgressed in this respect, they committed a sin beyond the power of Christ to pardon ? Grace has no limits. But there are limits to the sphere in which alone grace can act. Circumcision in itself was nothing ; but it was the mark of, and key to, a position of

apostle's aim is not at all to prove the truth of the resurrection by his appeal to nature, but to answer thereby the " fool's " objections against that truth : to show (I quote again from the same source) that in this matter " the system of religion, considered only as a system, and prior to the proof of it, is not a subject of ridicule unless that of nature be so too."

[1] 1 Cor. i. 17, 18, 23 ; ii. 1–6.   [2] Gal. v. 2.

privilege under covenant utterly inconsistent with grace. "The offence of the cross" was that it set aside every position of the kind ; not that it brought redemption through the death upon the tree, but that because it so brought redemption all were shut up to grace. If Paul had so preached Christ as to pay homage to human nature, and respect and accredit the vantage ground it claimed by virtue of its religion, persecution would have ceased, for the cross would have lost its offence.[1]

Redemption as preached by "the many" in Apostolic days brought no persecution, because it left man a platform on which "to make a fair show in the flesh." But the cross set aside the flesh altogether. If the death of Christ be preached as a means of salvation, not for lost sinners, but for the pious and devout, where is the offence ? But the cross comes in with its mighty power to bring low as well as to exalt, for it exalts none but those whom first it humbles. It calls upon the pious worshipper, if indeed he would have blessing, to come out from the shrine in which he trusts, and take his place in the market square beside the outcast and the vile. It tells the "earnest seeker" and the "anxious inquirer," that by their efforts they are only struggling out of the pit where alone grace can reach them. It proclaims to the worthy "communicant" of blameless life, whose mind is a treasury of orthodox doctrines, and whose ways are a pattern of all good, that he must come down and stand beside the drunkard and the harlot, there to receive salvation from the grace of God to the glory of God. They

[1] Gal. v. 11 : vi. 12.

who do thus preach the cross can testify that its offence has *not* ceased in our day and in our midst.

Redemption is not, first, an easy way of salvation for the sinner, and then a display of the character of God. God must be supreme. A man who makes self his chief aim is contemptible, but in the very nature of things God must be first in everything, else He would be no longer *God*. The obedience of Christ was infinitely precious to God, apart altogether from any results accruing to the sinner ; and the cross is the expression of that obedience tried to the utmost. In this light, His death was but the crowning act of a life yielded up to God. " He was obedient unto death, even the death of the cross "—the cross, as expressive beyond all else of agony and contempt to the full ; and because it was this, an expression too, the completest and most blessed, of perfect love to God and man. That death was but the climax of His life. It had another character, doubtless, in which it stands alone, for there divine judgment fell on Him for sin, and He became the outcast sin-offering. We do well, truly, at times to think thus of Calvary ; but we do not well to think only of it thus. The great burnt-offering aspect of the cross ought ever to be first, and never to be forgotten.[1]

[1] Even as we preach the sin-offering or the passover, the joy and strength of our own hearts ought to be the burnt-offering. And thus, whatever may be the results of our testimony, it will always be itself a continual burnt-offering, " a sweet savour of Christ unto God " (2 Cor. ii. 15). And the burnt-offering could never be accepted without the accompanying meat-offering. The work of Christ, even in its highest aspect, must never be separated from the intrinsic perfectness and majesty of His person. It was the burnt-offering with its meat-offering that Israel daily sacrificed to

And how we lower everything ! In the Jewish ritual we find the passover, the dedication of the covenant, and the sin-offering of the red heifer— the foundation sacrifices which were offered once for all. We have further the burnt-offering, the meat-offering, the peace-offering, and the great yearly sin-offering, besides others still of which I will make no mention here. Each one of all these many types has found its antitype in Christ ; but what do Christians know of them ? The passover alone would more than satisfy the gospel of to-day, and even that is humanised and lowered. Christ has died, and that is everything. How He died is scarce thought of, and Who He is who did so die is well-nigh forgotten altogether.[1] Christ has died

God ; and this aspect of the cross ought ever to be before us, and that for its own sake and not because of special need in us.

[1] The law of the leper may teach us a lesson here. Two sparrows were sold for a farthing, and no more was needed for the leper's cleansing. A farthing ! if price was to be paid at all, could it possibly be less ? It is impossible that the outcast sinner can have high or worthy thoughts of Christ, nor does God expect it from him. The acknowledgment of Him suffices, if only it be *true*, how poor and low soever it may be. The bitten Israelite who *looked* upon the brazen serpent lived ; '' as many as *touched* Him were made perfectly whole.'' It was only the leper's farthing offering, but it was enough. And so also now : '' whosoever shall call on the name of the Lord shall be saved,'' '' they that *hear* shall live.''

But after the sinner has been brought nigh to God, and found peace and pardon, and life, shall the poor estimate he formed of Christ and of His sacrifice, while yet an outcast, be still the limit of his gratitude, the measure of his worship ? Shall the *farthing* gospel that met the banished sinner's need, satisfy the heart of the citizen, the saint, the child of God ? The two sparrows restored the leper to the camp, but it then behoved him to bring *all* the great offerings of the law. Christ in all His fulness is God's provision for His people, and nothing less than this should be the measure of their hearts' worship (Lev. xiv.).

—that is certain. Rationalists and Ritualists, Protestants and Romanists, all are agreed that Christ has died. Whether it be in our Ragged Sunday schools, or in our Houses of Parliament, as day by day their sittings are begun by prayer, the death of Christ is a fact which need not be asserted, for none but an infidel would question it. But inquire in what way and to what extent sinners are benefited by that death, and at once the harmony is broken. Upon this every school has its creed, and every " ism " its theories, and the theme is the signal for a scramble and a struggle between all the rival banners of Christendom.

Here is a master-stroke of Satan's guile. That which God intended should be an impossibility to the natural mind, he has made the common creed of men. In the wildest fables of false religions, there is nothing more utterly incredible than the story of the life and death of the Son of God. For one who knows who Jesus was, and what " the Christ " means, to believe that Jesus is the Christ is so entirely beyond the possibilities of human reason that it is proof of a birth from God.[1] He who believes that Jesus is the Son of God is a man with a supernatural faith, a faith that overcomes the world.[2] Yet just as in Him the carnal eye could find no beauty,[3] so in His gospel the carnal mind can see no wonders. But it behoves the evangelist so to preach that gospel that the Holy Ghost may own the word to reveal thereby the mighty mysteries and marvels of redemption ; not lowering and humanising it to bring it within the reach of the

[1] 1 John v. 1.   [2] 1 John v. 5.   [3] Isa. liii. 2 ; Mark vi. 3.

natural man apart from the work of the Holy Spirit.[1]

If Christians are commonplace in our day, may it not be because the gospel they believe is commonplace ? Divine faith is faith in the divine. The difference is not in the faith, but in the object of it. If we have really believed the Gospel of God, we have each one of us received for himself a revelation from on high, a revelation to which flesh and blood could never reach. Let us remember this. These pages are proof how much I value clear and scriptural statements of the truth ; but it is not on clearness, or even orthodoxy, that the *power* depends. The gospel may be so sifted and simplified that none shall fail to understand it, and yet sinners may never be brought to God at all. The preaching that is wanted is not " with persuasive words of man's wisdom," reasoning out salvation, and cheapening the gospel to suit the condition of the hearers, but " *in demonstration of the Spirit and of power* " —preaching that will be " foolishness to them that perish," but to the saved " the power of God."

It is one thing to master Christianity ; it is quite another thing to be mastered by it. And it is the cross that attracts and conquers. The cross, not as an easy way of pardon for the sinner, not as a " plan of salvation," but as a fact and a revelation to change a heartless worldling into an adoring worshipper. The cross, not as the ruling factor in the equation of man's redemption, but as

[1] Some preachers seem to bring Christ to the sinner, but the true evangelist brings the sinner to Christ—in other words, Christ and not the sinner is the central object in his testimony.

a display of the love and righteousness and wrath of God, and the sin of man, to subdue the hardest heart, and change the whole current of the most selfish and ungodly life.

To faith the unseen is real ; and to those who believe in the cross, " Jesus Christ has been openly set forth crucified before their eyes." [1] They have seen that marred and agonised face. They have been witnesses to the reproach that broke His heart, the scorn, the derision, and the hate, of all the attendant throng. They have heard " Emmanuel's orphan cry " when forsaken of His God. And in gazing thus upon that scene their inmost being has sustained a mighty change. Till yesterday, the world and self ensnared their hearts, and filled the whole horizon of their lives. But now the cross has become a power to divorce themselves from self, and to separate them from that world which crucified their Lord.

O for power so to preach the cross of Christ that it shall become a reality to all, whether they accept it or despise it : that men who never were conscious of a doubt, because they never really *believed*, shall see what priests and soldiers saw, and the rabble crowd that mocked His agonies, and seeing, shall exclaim, " It is impossible that this can be the Son of God ! " that some again shall see what John and Mary witnessed, and gazing, shall cry out, with broken hearts, in mingled love and grief, " My God, was this for me ! " and turn to live devoted lives for Him who died and rose again.

I conclude in borrowed words, more worthy than

[1] Gal. iii. 1, R.V.

my own : " With the loyal-hearted believer, there
is one master-object which in measure conceals
every other by its surpassing glory ; and this is not
redemption, which, blessed as it is, is simply a
matter of course, *if Christ died for this end*, but the
CROSS itself, with its ignominy—the death of the
Prince of Life, the crucifixion of the Lord of Glory :
incredible antithesis ! Not only the freedom from
eternal and frightful slavery, but the divine price
paid for that freedom. And this ' not silver and
gold ' (though we were not worth so much as brass),
but ' the precious blood of Christ.'

" And so I would preach to those who hear, and
say ' There is life, there is pardon, there is righteousness for you—nay, there is worth for you—
and they are all Divine, besides their own integrity ;
and they are a free gift to the godless and lost. But
I tell you more, and beg you to hasten on ; this
life, these riches, come to you through His poverty
and death ; and God and God's love are revealed
to you in this poverty, this death, even the death
of the cross.'

" And if I were to tell you of forgiveness of sins
through His mercy, and leave you there ; if I
preached to you the results flowing of necessity
from the cross to each believer, but not the cross
itself, or the cross itself as a judicial work, but not
the Crucified One, I should leave you still to self,
and I desire to save you from self, as well as from
everlasting shame and contempt. But I preach
Christ Jesus the Lord, the Son of God, the bright-
ness of His glory and express image of Himself,
on the cross made a curse and smitten there by the

hand of God judicially for the guilty. See the dreadfulness of that cross, and know who it is that was lifted up on it, and for whom, and to what end, as it is written. Look steadily ; mark, study, search into those unsearchable moral riches ; and blessing after blessing will come to you, and so freely, from this one object, in which all truth and all love are alike declared, and in which you will learn to love, to worship and to obey, to abhor wrong, to forget yourself and think of Him, and to ' count all things but loss,' as the apostle says, not for the grace of your deliverance, but ' for the excellency of the knowledge of Christ Jesus your Lord.' "

4

FAITH

FAITH is a mystery to many, a stumbling-block
to not a few. By some it seems to be regarded as
the condition upon which God compounds with men
who ought to have righteousness, but have it not :
with others it is the last mite added to make up the
price of our redemption. At times it appears like
a new barrier set up between the soul and God,
when the work of Christ had broken all the old
barriers down ; and not unfrequently it is represented as an operation, like the new birth itself,
in which the sinner is a passive agent in the hands
of God. There is the rationalist view of faith,
making it merely the assent of the mind to truth
demonstratively proved ; there is the Romanist
view of faith, which makes it a sort of good work
of a mystical and spiritual kind ; and again, there is
what I may term the fatalist theory of faith, which
regards it as a kind of grace imparted to the soul
by God.

But when we turn to Scripture all such subtleties
and errors vanish like mists before the sun. " Faith
cometh by hearing, and hearing by the Word of
God." [1] What simplicity, and yet what reality

[1] Rom. x. 17.

and power are here! " Faith cometh by hearing," whether it be faith of the gospel, or of the news of some temporal calamity or good. There are no two ways of believing anything. And hearing comes—the true hearing—by the Word of God : not by reasonings founded on it, it may be rightly founded on it ; not by " enticing words of man's wisdom,"[1] but by the Word of God. And here is where the difference lies, not in the character of the faith, but in the object of it. The sinner is brought into the presence of God. He hears *God*, he believes *God*, and he is blest with believing Abraham, and just on the same ground, for " Abraham *believed God*, and it was reckoned unto him for righteousness."[2]

In its first and simplest phase in Scripture, faith is the belief of a record or testimony ; it is, secondly, belief in a person ; and it has, lastly, the character of trust, which always points to what is future. To speak of trust as the only true phase of gospel faith, is wholly false and wrong. In fact, the word generally rendered " trust," is never used in this connection once in Scripture. It is etymologically " hope," and the element of hope invariably enters into it. In what is pre-eminently the gospel book of the Bible, it occurs but once,[3] and in the sermons of the Acts we shall seek for it in vain. " We are saved by trust," is a statement at once true and scriptural, if only we understand salvation in its fullest sense, as yet to be made good to us in glory ;[4] but the salvation of our souls[5] is not matter of trust, but of faith in its simplest form. The redemption

[1] 1 Cor. ii. 4. [2] Rom. iv. 3, R.V. [6] John v. 45.
[4] Rom. viii. 24. [5] 1 Pet. i. 9.

of our souls is a fact to us, because we believe the record God has given of His Son , no less so is the redemption of our bodies, but it is because of our trust in God. As the apostle writes to Timothy, " We *trust* in the living God, who is the Saviour of all men, especially of those that *believe*." [1] Trust springs from confidence in the person trusted , and that again depends on knowledge of the person confided in. In this sense, faith may be great or little, weak or strong " I write unto you, little children " (says the Apostle John), " because your sins are forgiven you for His name's sake." [2] Here is a testimony and a fact. Upon our state of soul may depend the realisation, the enjoyment of it, but this faith can admit of no degrees. But trust in God has as many degrees as there are saints on earth. Some believers could not trust Him for a single meal others can look to Him, without misgivings, to feed a thousand hungry mouths, or to convert a thousand godless sinners. Our faith in this sense, depends entirely on knowing God, and on communion with Him , the faith of the gospel comes by *hearing* Him.[3]

At every pier along the new embankment of the Thames, there hangs a chain that reaches to the water's edge at its lowest ebb But for this, some poor creature, struggling with death, might drown with his very hand upon the pier An appeal

[1] 1 Tim. iv. 10. See the use of the same word in 1 Tim iii. 14 ; v. 5 , vi. 17.

[2] 1 John ii 12

[3] So much so, that hearing is sometimes taken to include faith, as, *e.g.*, John v. 25, and Col. i. 6. The gospel brought forth fruit in Colosse " from the day they *heard* it "

to perishing sinners to trust in Christ is like calling
on a drowning wretch to climb the embankment
wall. The glad tidings, the testimony of God
concerning Christ, is the chain let down for the
hand of faith to grasp.[1] Once rescued, it is not
the chain the river waif would trust for safety, but
the rock beneath his feet ; yet, but for that chain,
the rock might have only mocked his struggles.
And it is not the gospel message the ransomed sinner
trusts in, but the living Christ of whom the gospel
speaks ; but yet it was the message that his faith
at first laid hold upon, and by it he gained an eternal
standing-ground upon the Rock of Ages.

He who truly hears the good news of Christ
believes it just as the little child believes a mother's
word. And none but such shall ever enter the
kingdom.[2] There is neither mystery nor virtue
in the faith, in the one case any more than in the
other ; the only difference is in the testimony itself.
He who believes the gospel, receives a word that is
nothing less than " the power of God unto salvation." [3] If, in fact, none can believe apart from the
work of the Holy Spirit, the difficulty depends on
no peculiarity in the faith itself. It is not a question of metaphysics, but of spiritual depravity
and death. As far as the act of faith is concerned,
the gospel is believed in the same way as the passing

---

[1] The case of Cornelius affords a striking example of this. " A
devout man, and one that feared God with all his house, and prayed
to God alway," it might well be asked, What did he lack ? Yet
to such an one the message came : " Send men to Joppa and call
for Simon Peter, who shall tell thee *words* whereby thou and all
thy house shall be saved " (Acts xi. 13, 14).

[2] Luke xviii. 17.   [3] Rom. i. 16.

news of the passing hour. The hindrance lies in the apostasy of the natural heart of man. And, doubtless, the reason faith is made the turning point of the sinner's return to God is just because distrust was the turning point of his departure from Him.[1] Disobedience was not the first step in Adam's fall ; it was the last, and it followed upon disbelief.

Faith then in its simplest character is not trust, nor even faith in a person, but belief of a record. "Whosoever believeth that Jesus is the Christ, is born of God." "Who is he that overcometh the world, but he that believeth that Jesus is the Son of God ? " And so, if we read through the chapter from which these words are quoted, we find it is the witness, or testimony of God, that is in question between the sinner and Himself. "There are three who bear witness, the Spirit and the water and the blood ; and the three agree in one. If we receive the witness of men, the witness of God is greater ; for the witness of God is this, that He hath borne witness concerning His Son. He that believeth on the Son of God hath the witness in himself.[2] He that believeth not God hath made Him a liar, because he hath not believed in the witness that God hath borne concerning His Son." [3] And so

[1] See chap. xi. *post.*

[2] *I.e.*, it is no longer something in a book merely, outside himself, but it has become identified with the believer, and is part of his very being. Compare Jer. xv. 16, John v. 38, etc.

[3] I John v. 8–11, R.V. In the whole passage, beginning with verse 6, the terms "water" and "blood" are to be interpreted by the typology of Scripture. Christ came as the fulfilment not merely of "the water of purification" (Num. xix.), but of "the blood of atonement" (Lev. xvi.).

also if we turn to the Gospel of John. The Book was written that we might believe " that Jesus is the Christ, the Son of God ; and that, believing, we might have life through His name.[1]

Nor will this seem strange to any who understand the gospel. The gospel is not a promise or a covenant, but a message, a proclamation.[2] It is the " good news of God, concerning His Son Jesus Christ our Lord." [3] And the belief of that good news is life : not indeed when retailed as the word of man, to suit the whims or errors of the natural heart, but when it comes in the power of the Holy Ghost, and, " as it is in truth, the word of God." " The *words* that I have spoken unto you, they are spirit and they are life," the Lord declared, when many of His disciples were offended at His teaching. The many heard but the words of Jesus the Nazarene, and were offended and went back. To the few, these same words were " words of eternal life," and called forth the confession of Him as Christ the Son of God.[4]

The 10th chapter of Romans claims notice here, confirming, as it does so fully, what the other Scriptures already quoted amply prove. God has brought the gospel as near to men as in the old time He brought the law. " This commandment which I command thee this day, it is not hidden from thee, neither is it far off," said Moses in his parting charge to Israel,[5]—" It is not in heaven, that thou shouldest say, Who shall go up for us to heaven, and bring it unto us, that we may hear it and do it ? Neither

[1] John xx. 31.　　[2] See *e.g.*, 1 Cor. xv. 1–4 ; Acts xiii. 38, 39.
[3] Rom i. 1, 3.　　[4] John vi. 69.　　[5] Deut. xxx. 11–14.

is it beyond the sea, that thou shouldest say,
Who shall go over the sea for us, and bring
it unto us, that we may hear it and do it ?
But the word is very nigh unto thee, in thy
mouth, and in thy heart, that thou mayest do
it."

Thus spake the righteousness of law , now, hear
the righteousness of faith " Say not in thine
heart, Who shall ascend into heaven ? (that is, to
bring Christ down from above) or, Who shall
descend into the deep ? (that is, to bring up Christ
again from the dead) But what saith it ? The
word is nigh thee, even in thy mouth and in thy
heart : that is, the word of faith, which we preach ,
that if thou shalt confess with thy mouth the Lord
Jesus, and shalt believe in thine heart that God
hath raised Him from the dead, thou shalt be
saved." [1] It was for Israel to have the commandment in their mouth, and to do it with their heart ,
it is ours to have the gospel in our mouth, and to
believe it with our heart. There is no mystery
in the one case any more than in the other Metaphysical distinctions between believing with the
head and with the heart, are wholly untenable
A Christian believes with his heart, just as a Jew
obeyed with his heart. It was the obedience of
the inner man, the real man, that God required ,
and so it is with faith

In modern English " the heart " is synonymous
with the affections ; but not in Scripture The
Lord speaks of " the heart " as the moral being,
the true man as distinguished from the mere out-

[1] Rom x. 6–10.

ward man.[1] And so also here. With the mouth man speaks, but the confession of the lip may or may not be the expression of what is within, and therefore secret. The confession of Christ by the outward man is the sequel and complement of the faith of the inward man. A man cannot believe with his affections; indeed, all such expressions are fanciful. Love and hope and faith and fear are not independent entities with rival or co-ordinate rank in the complex being, man. It is the man himself who loves, and hopes, and believes, and fears. Just as he may say he loves, and never love at all, so he may say he believes, and the profession may be a sham ; but if he really believes,[2] and believes *God*, the gift of God is his. But there is no subtlety in the faith. " Faith comes by hearing " ; faith in God comes by hearing God. " Every one that hath heard from the Father,"—said the Lord Himself, or perhaps, making due allowance for the English idiom, the verse would be better rendered, " Every one that hath heard the Father, and hath learned of Him, cometh unto Me." But as for them to whom He spoke, they *could* not hear.[3]

[1] Mark vii. 18–23. The *mind* is so used elsewhere. See p. 60 *post*.

[2] " Not, to be sure, in a speculative, but in a practical sense."— BISHOP BUTLER.

[3] John vi. 45, and viii. 43. Some men speak of the Spirit's work in the soul, as though the sinner were an irresponsible vessel which God fills with faith ; and yet these same men, when faith itself becomes their theme, seem to forget the Spirit's work entirely, and enlarge on subtle distinctions between head faith and heart faith, " faith in " and " faith on," faith of *saving* truth, and faith in general, until faith itself looms great and mysterious upon the burdened sinner, shutting Christ out altogether.

Let us then get this great fact implanted firmly in our minds, that there is neither merit nor virtue in faith, nor even in the letter of the truth believed ; but that *to believe God* is eternal life. To believe God, whether it be, as with Abraham, the promise of a family,[1] or, as with us, the testimony to a Person and a fact. Faith is the opened lattice that lets in the light of heaven to the soul, bringing gladness and blessing with it. It is only in ophthalmic hospitals that people are always thinking of their eyes, and it is due entirely to the prevailing errors and follies of modern teaching that so many Christians are hypochondriacs respecting faith. In Scripture, faith is like healthy eyesight, unheeded and forgotten in the ease and enjoyment of its use. Nowadays it is more like the glasses of people with failing or defective vision, sometimes lost, often dim, and constantly a trouble.

But faith not only receives the word of Christ ; it reaches on, and lays hold upon the person of Christ. Belief of His word leads to belief in Himself. And here, again, there is no difficulty, save such as men have made. To receive Christ, to come to Christ, to believe in Christ—for all these words are used in Scripture—means to-day just what it meant when the Lord was living upon earth. To come to Christ, was not outward contact with the son of Mary, but submission of heart to the Son of God. " No man can come to Me except the Father draw him," was His word to those who had followed Him from Capernaum to Tiberias, and back again across the sea. Anyone might come to Jesus, and

[1] Gen. xv. 5, 6.

none need leave His presence without proof of His
power and grace. He fed the hungry just because
they hungered. He healed the oppressed of Satan,
just because they were oppressed, and His mission
was to destroy the devil's work. But how few
there were of those who thus came to Jesus, that
ever truly came to Christ!

" If ye believe not that I am He, ye shall die in
your sins." " That I am He " : it was this that
faith laid hold upon. They who did believe it as a
divine revelation came to believe in Himself in a
further and fuller sense, and this again led to confidence and trust, just in proportion as they were
abiding in Him, and His word in them, and, moreover, as their knowledge of Him increased. " How
is it that ye have no faith ? " was the Lord's appeal
to the terrified disciples on the Sea of Galilee, when
they awoke Him with upbraidings for neglecting
them. In the gospel sense they believed on Him
then, as they ever did ; and indeed their remon-
strances were based on their unchanging confidence
that, being the Christ the Son of God, He had power
to deliver them, but did not. They believed on
Him, but as yet they did not *know* Him, and therefore their knowledge of His power only led them to
doubt His love.

" Acquaint now thyself with Him and be at
peace," [1] is a word for the tempest-tossed believer.
The faith that " comes by hearing," brings us
salvation and the knowledge of salvation. The
faith that springs from abiding in Him and acquaint-
ing ourselves with Him, is the secret of a peace-

[1] Job xxii. 21.

ruled heart and a holy life Like all the sons of faith, Saul of Tarsus believed God, and so set out upon the Christian course And the ' faithful saying '' that brought life and joy to him at the starting-post, was the strength of his heart even to the goal [1] It is the same gospel that is the resting-place for our feet as we lay hold upon the Rock of Ages, which becomes the pillow of our dying hour as we pass away from our service and our sins on earth Whether as the converted persecutor on the Damascus road, or as the Apostle of the Lord at the close of that matchless life of labour and testimony, Paul's faith in the gospel was the same. Here it is not growth we speak of, but steadfastness [2] At the beginning, just as at the end of his race, he " believed God," but at the end, when looking back upon his life from his Roman prison, he could add, " I *know* whom I have believed " , and having come to know Him, he had learned to trust Him

Everybody understands what it means to believe in the claimant of a fortune or a title It is just to receive him for what he represents himself to be. And believing in Christ means primarily nothing more than this It leads to more, doubtless , but that depends not on any peculiarity or virtue in the faith, but on Him who is the object of faith They who thus believe in the Lord Jesus come to confide in Him, to trust Him, and to love Him , but to believe on Him is simply to " receive His testimony," and thus to " set to our seal that God is true." [3] And yet, such faith is impossible apart from the work of the Holy Spirit in the soul " Whoso-

[1] 1 Tim i. 15   [2] Col. ii. 5   [3] John iii 33, 36

ever believeth that Jesus is the Christ *is born of God*." Not, I repeat again, for it needs to be repeated, that faith in Christ is a metaphysical achievement so difficult that man is insufficient to accomplish it ; but that the heart is utterly apostate, and man's natural condition is that of pure distrust of God.

More than this, " the carnal mind is enmity against God." [1] Man is capable of the firmest and most implicit faith in himself and in the world— aye, and in the devil too, as will be proved one day ; but his whole spiritual being is so utterly estranged from God that not only does he not know Him, but, if left to himself, he is incapable of knowing Him. Just as a warped window-pane distorts all objects seen through it, so the human heart perverts even the very truth of God, and changes it into a lie.[2] A heart in fellowship with God would have found proof in every act and word of Christ that He was divine ; but men heard His words and saw His works—sincere men, too, and good and estimable — and yet adjudged Him to be an impostor. *Because* He told them the truth, they believed Him not.[3] And as it was then, so is it still. It is not the head that is at fault, but the heart ; it is not that man is silly, but that he is sinful ; not that he is weak, but that he is wicked.

Indeed, if Christians were made, as certain writers upon evidences would lead us to suppose, by reasoning out Christianity from the miracles of Christ, the company of the Lord's disciples would have numbered thousands more than the little band

[1] Rom. viii. 7. [2] Rom. i. 25. [3] John viii. 45.

who owned His name. Those who believed on Him thus were not few, but many. But He who could judge the heart refused to commit Himself to such.[1] The true faith is not based on " evidences," but on the word of God ; and these miracle-made believers could not and would not hear that word.[2] To acknowledge Jesus of Nazareth as the promised Son of David, on account of the miracles He did, was one thing ; to receive eternal life in Christ was quite apart from it.

There had never risen a greater prophet than John the Baptist ; and yet at the very time this testimony was given to him, his *political* faith, if I may use the expression, had broken down, and his disciples were on their way back to his prison, to reassure him by the record of the Lord's miracles.[3] And so it was at the last with His most favoured saints : " We trusted that it had been He which should have redeemed Israel," was their sad tribute to the memory of His name. Their faith had failed, their hope had died out, leaving only love to cling to Him ; but still they were His own. In common with the multitude around them, they had seen His miracles, and hailed Him as their coming king. But more than this, they had themselves been the subjects of a miracle the multitude knew nothing of : they had been born again by the word of Him whom now they mourned. They had received the gift of life from God ; and though they knew it not, that death which seemed to them the end of all their hopes secured to them eternal glory.

[1] John ii. 23, 24 ; and comp. John vii. 31 with viii. 30–47.
[2] John viii. 43, 47. And see Appendix, Note I. [3] Matt. xi. 2–6.

" However," says Bishop Butler in summing up his argument on this point, " the fact is allowed that Christianity was professed to be received into the world upon the belief of miracles," and " that is what its first converts would have alleged as their reason for embracing it." [1] True it is that no earnest, honest man, with the Scriptures at hand, could doubt the Messiahship of Jesus, while witnessing the miracles He wrought ; but it is no less true that men cannot reason themselves into Christianity. How different from Butler's account of it, is the story the early Christians told of their conversion ! What is the testimony of those who were with Him in the Holy Mount, and witnessed that greatest miracle of all ? " Which were born," writes the beloved disciple, " not of blood, nor of the will of the flesh, nor of the will of man, but of God." [2] " Being born again, not of corruptible seed, but of incorruptible, by the word of God, which liveth and abideth for ever," is the kindred witness of the Apostle Peter.[3]

Nor did Paul, as great a reasoner as Butler, strike a discordant note : " God, who commanded the light to shine out of darkness, hath shined in our hearts." [4] Such was his glad but humble testimony. The multitudes followed Him because of the loaves His power supplied : *they* cared not for the bread of heaven. But His true disciples knew and owned Him as the One who had the words of eternal life. This was the bond that kept them at His side when the many were offended and drew

---

[1] *The Analogy*, pt. 2, ch. vii. sec. 3.   [2] John i. 13.
[3] 1 Pet. i. 23.   [4] 2 Cor. iv. 6.

back. The works of God might convince the reason; but it was not thus the dead got life, the troubled conscience peace. To weigh the evidences and embrace Christianity, as the true religion, is the part of a fair and prudent man; but salvation is God's work altogether. The blessing is not for the apt scholar, but for the outcast and lost. It is not for the clear head, but for the contrite heart. Not for the clever reasoner, but for the self-judged and guilty; not for logicians, but for sinners; not for the wise and prudent, but for babes.

So it has been in every age. The public revelation of God to man has varied again and again, but His secret revelation to the soul that turns to Him has ever been the same. "He brought me up out of a horrible pit, out of the miry clay, and set my feet upon a rock, and established my goings, and He hath put a new song in my mouth." [1] Thus sang His saints in the old days three thousand years ago; so sing they still. "It pleased God to reveal His Son in me," is the testimony of Paul; [2] and if Peter owned Him as the Son of the living God, it was not a deduction from His miracles, but a revelation from the Father in heaven. [3] And so with the rest. It was not that they saw His works, but that they heard His words. [4]

We are saved by *faith*; and faith is the reception, as true, of what is beyond the range of proof, either by demonstration or by evidence. It is the

---

[1] Ps. xl. 2, 3.   [2] Gal. i. 15, 16.   [3] Matt. xvi. 17.
[4] " I have given unto them the *words* which Thou gavest Me; and they have received them " (John xvii. 8).

substance (or assurance) of things hoped or trusted for, the conviction of things not seen.[1] Salvation is within the reach of all, but it is as suppliant sinners they must receive it. Grace does not place either the Saviour or the Gospel at the bar of human judgment; *that* is the arrogance of infidelity. As has been already seen, grace is based upon the cross, and assumes that man is guilty and lost. It does not place him in the dock, but it finds him there : it does not brand him as ruined and lost, but it comes to him as thus branded already. And the very gospel which tells of life and peace and pardon, is itself the power to make good this testimony. It is not a question of God's submitting either Himself or His revelation to the tribunal of the creature's judgment, but of the sinner's waking up from his death-sleep in sin to hear the voice of God. The hour is come of which it is written, " The dead shall hear the voice of the Son of God, and they that *hear* shall live." [2]

We are saved through faith, but faith is not our saviour. If faith had intrinsic virtue and could bring blessing with it, hell would be impossible ; for there are no unbelievers save on earth, and that, too, in the days of Christ's humiliation and His absence. The day is coming when all shall believe and confess His name. And if faith and confession bring blessing now, it is not because of any merit they possess, but because God is saving men in sovereign grace. . If the blessing were not by grace, it never could be gained by such as we are. " Therefore it is of faith, that it might be by

[1] Heb. xi. 1.   [2] John v. 25.

grace." [1]   As it is written, " By grace are ye saved
through faith ; and that (salvation) not of yourselves, it is the gift of God." [2]   Salvation is the
gift of God, bestowed on the principle of grace,
and received on the principle of faith.

And how does faith come ?   " Faith cometh
by hearing, and hearing by the word of God." [3]
This is the time of which Isaiah spoke, when God
is found of them that seek Him not ; [4] the time
in which the gospel is to be carried to the lanes and
highways of the world, and men are to be compelled
to come in ; [5] when forgiveness of sins is to be proclaimed far and wide, and all that believe are
justified ; when there is salvation for the lost, life
for the dead, heaven for the outcast sinner.   The
cross has been set up, not half-way on the road to

[1] Rom. iv. 16.

[2] Eph. ii. 8.   " The gift of God " here is *salvation by grace
through faith*.   Not the faith itself.   " This is precluded," as Alford
remarks, "by the manifestly parallel clauses 'not of yourselves,'
and ' not of works,' the latter of which would be irrelevant as
asserted of *faith*."   It is still more definitely precluded, he might
have added, by the character of the passage.   It is *given* to us to
believe on Christ, just in the same sense in which it is given to some
" also to suffer for His sake " (Phil. i. 29).   But the statement
in Ephesians is *doctrinal*, and in that sense the assertion that faith
is a gift, or indeed that it is a distinct entity at all, is sheer error.
This matter is sometimes represented as though God gave faith
to the sinner first, and then, on the sinner's bringing Him the faith,
went on and gave him salvation !   Just as though a baker, refusing
to supply empty-handed applicants, should first dispense to each
the price of a loaf, and then, in return for the money from his own
till, serve out the bread !   To answer fully such a vagary as this
would be to rewrite the foregoing chapter.   Suffice it, therefore, to
point out that to read the text as though faith were the gift, is to
destroy not only the meaning of verse 9, but the force of the whole
passage.

[3] Rom. x. 17.   [4] Rom. x. 20.   [5] Luke xiv. 23.

heaven, where man's unbelieving heart would place it, but right down in the market square of the City of Destruction, that men may look and live. Such are " the exceeding riches of His grace in His kindness toward us through Christ Jesus."

5

REPENTANCE and the SPIRIT'S WORK

PAGAN mythology had a three-headed monster at the door of hell, but modern Christianity has its *Cerberus* at the gate of heaven. Faith, repentance, and the Spirit's work, by God intended to bring salvation to our very door, are turned by men into a threefold hindrance on the way to life. Or, to change the figure, faith is a rugged mountain on the pilgrim's path, and repentance a dreary slough beyond it. The mountain and the marsh are passed in safety, only to find perplexities more hopeless still ; for the fickle phantom of the Spirit's work must then be grasped and made his own, before the pilgrim can cross the threshold of the pearly gate. What a burlesque upon the gospel !

From the twilight days of prophetic testimony a divine voice still vibrates in our air, " As I LIVE, saith the Lord God, I HAVE NO PLEASURE IN THE DEATH OF THE WICKED." And turning to the clearer light and surer word of Him who came to give a ghastly but most blessed proof of the deep meaning of God's great oath, we gaze on Calvary, and as we gaze and worship, the words seem written there in judgment fire and redeeming blood : " GOD SO LOVED THE WORLD THAT HE GAVE HIS ONLY-

BEGOTTEN SON." Every fact and testimony of the gospel assures, and is intended to convince us, that God is on the sinner's side, and " will have all men to be saved, and to come unto the knowledge of the truth." [1] Is the case so hopeless that man can do absolutely nothing for himself ? Then righteousness is " to him that worketh *not* but believeth " ; " It is of faith that it may be by grace." [2] Is man so utterly at enmity that even this would not suffice ? The Holy Ghost has come down from heaven to turn our hearts to God and to secure to us every blessing Christ has won.

But here I have spoken only of faith and the Spirit's work : what then about repentance ? Are faith and the Spirit's work enough ? or is not repentance no less a necessity, if men are to be saved ? I meet this question boldly and at once by denouncing it as based, not so much on ignorance as on deep-seated and systematic error. The repentance which thus obtrudes itself and claims notice in every sermon is not the friend of the gospel, but an enemy. It is like the officious guide who forces himself upon the traveller only to mislead him. Faith and repentance are not successive stages on the road to life ; they are not independent guides to direct the pilgrim's path ; they are not separate acts to be successively accomplished by the sinner as a condition of his salvation. But, in different phases of it, they represent the same Godward attitude of soul, which the truth of God, believed, produces.

Salvation there cannot be without repentance,

[1] 1 Tim. ii. 4.　　　　[2] Rom. iv. 5, 16.

any more than without faith ; but the soundest and fullest gospel - preaching need not include any mention of the word. Neither as verb nor noun does it occur in the Epistle to the Romans—God's great doctrinal treatise on redemption and righteousness—save in the warnings of the 2nd chapter. And the Gospel of John—pre-eminently the gospel· book of the Bible—will be searched in vain for a single mention of it. The beloved disciple wrote his Gospel, that men might believe and live,[1] and his Epistle followed, to confirm believers in the simplicity and certainty of their faith ; [2] but yet, from end to end of them, the word " repent " or " repentance " never once occurs.[3] It is to these writings, before all others, that men have turned in every age to find words of peace and life ; and yet some who profess to hold them as inspired will cavil at a gospel sermon because repentance is not mentioned in it : a fault, if fault it be, that marks the testimony of the Apostle John, and the preaching of our Lord Himself, as recorded by the Fourth Evangelist. The repentance of the gospel is to be found in the Nicodemus sermon, and in the gracious

---

[1] John xx. 31.   [2] 1 John v. 13.

[3] This is the more remarkable from the fact that the word occurs so often in the Revelation. Any one can verify my statement by the help of a concordance. The word is used 58 times in the New Testament. Of these, 25 are to be ascribed to Luke in his Gospel and the Acts, and 12 to the Apocalypse. Paul uses it but 5 times.

μεταμέλομαι is used in Matt. xxi. 29, 32 ; xxvii. 3 ; 2 Cor. vii. 8 ; and Heb. vii. 21. In 2 Cor. vii. both words are rendered " repent " in the Authorised Version. The revisers read the passage : " I do not regret it though I did regret .   . ye were made sorry to repentance . . . godly sorrow worketh repentance unto salvation, a repentance which bringeth no regret."

testimony to the woman at the well. And, I may add, any repentance that limits or jars upon those sacred words, is wholly against the truth.

What then is repentance ? The question, bear in mind, concerns the truth of God and our own salvation. It is not a problem in etymology. Etymologically, *metanoia* in Greek, and repentance in English, have exactly the same significance— an after-mind, the result of second thoughts or reflection. Moreover, the word in Greek is often used in this its primary sense. But second thoughts too often involve regret, and not unfrequently remorse ; and it will not seem strange to any who have studied the history of words that *metanoia* should have come to cover the entire range of meaning, from mere change of mind to sorrow and remorse. Our task is therefore to turn to Holy Writ, and, comparing Scripture with Scripture, to discover what *God* means when He calls men to repentance.

And here we do well to bear in mind a canon of interpretation, given specially regarding prophecy, but true of revelation as a whole. No passage of Scripture is to be isolated, and explained apart from other Scriptures.[1] The words are to be interpreted consistently with what the Holy Spirit has elsewhere revealed. Taking heed then to the two rival errors, toward one or other of which our creeds are always tending, we can clear the ground at once by deciding that repentance does not mean penitence or sorrow, or any condition of soul or change of heart that makes the sinner acceptable

[1] 2 Pet. i. 20.

to God, or has merit of its own. The Romanist view of repentance we reject at once, as opposed to the doctrinal teaching of the Epistle to the Romans, and the plain testimony of the Fourth Evangelist. Whatever repentance means, it must be something consistent with grace, and something implied in the Gospel of John.

But while refusing to exalt repentance at the cost of grace, we must guard against the Rationalist extreme of reducing it to a mere mental change.[1] Much of what I have said respecting faith might well be repeated here. God must have reality. If He demands " a change of *mind*," it is not of the intellectual faculty He speaks, but of the man himself, the real man. So the apostle uses the word in the Epistle to the Romans and elsewhere, " I myself, with the mind, serve the law of God." [2] Repentance is the turning of the mind or heart— the man *himself*.

Repentance is not faith, nor faith repentance ; but yet they are inseparable. Inseparable, that is, in connection with the gospel. Therefore it is that the word " repent " is so seldom used in the sermons of the New Testament, and also that it sometimes stands alone as the principle on which man receives the blessing. " He that believeth hath," implies

[1] It is but natural that the recoil from what I have termed " the Romanist view of repentance " should have carried men into extremes ; and at this moment there is some danger of a reaction toward the old error of the *Douay* Bible, which confounds repentance with *penitence*. But the true antidote to the prevailing levity of the day is not a return to legality in preaching, but a more just appreciation of the solemnity of grace, and a worthier testimony to the greatness and majesty of the God with whom we have to do.

[2] Rom. vii. 25 ; and see page 44 *ante*.

repentance ; "repent and be converted," involves faith. The hand that clutches the assassin's knife must open ere it can grasp the gift its intended victim proffers ; and opening that hand, though a single act, has a double aspect and purpose. Accepting the gift implies a turning from the crime on which the heart was bent, and it was the gift itself that worked the change. Faith is the open hand, relatively to the gift ; repentance is the same hand, relatively, not only to the gift, but more especially to the dagger it has flung from it.

The schoolmen would explain that, chronologically, faith comes first, and then, repentance ; but that, in their logical order, repentance has precedence. But the question of priority, though an interesting problem in metaphysics, is a profitless study in theology. Practically, they are simultaneous. He who truly believes in the Lord Jesus Christ may rest assured that he has repented ; and "repentance toward God" equally implies "faith toward our Lord Jesus Christ."[1] That is, under the preaching of the gospel. Judgment-warnings might produce repentance, as Jonah's preaching did at Nineveh ; but in the gospel, it is not the wrath, but the goodness of God, that leads to it.[2]

Repentance, as I have said, has a twofold bearing. The characteristic of gospel repentance is repentance *to* ; under the past dispensation, it was repentance *from*. John the Baptist, for instance, preached repentance in order to faith in One then yet to come. A man is crossing a moor at night, his eye fixed upon a light that marks, as he supposes,

[1] Acts xx. 21. [2] Rom. ii. 4.

the homestead of a friend. Presently he meets another traveller, belated like himself, who tells him that the light he has been pressing towards is nothing but a gipsy's tent. As for the house he seeks, the stranger only knows that it is in a different direction altogether, but where, he cannot say ; a shepherd will soon be passing who knows it well. Convinced of his mistake, he turns from the path he has been following, and sits down upon a stone to await the coming of the expected guide. Such was the repentance the Baptist preached, a repentance from dead works, in order that they should believe in Him which should come after Him.[1] But the full gospel of Christ is like a friend who meets the erring wanderer, and, by the same testimony that convinces him he is on a wrong path, turns him to the destination which he seeks.

According to an ingenious derivation suggested for it, the Greek word for " man " implies a face turned upwards. And such, in a moral sense, is the normal condition of the creature ; such was Adam as he came from the hand of God. But sin brought in estrangement ; and our race springs, not from Adam in Eden innocence, but from the fallen outcast. By nature man's face is now averted from his God.[2] He needs, therefore, to be turned right round again. There is no difficulty here save such as theology has made. The student of Scripture finds there, in clear and simple language, what every one who has a spiritual history has learned as plainly from his own heart, that man by nature gravitates from God ; spiritually " his

[1] Acts xix. 4.   [2] Man's *natural* condition is now *abnormal*

countenance is fallen," his back is turned upon his Maker. The need, therefore, is not that he should mend his ways, but that he should change his course altogether.

The traveller's gait may be slovenly, and his pace slow ; yet little does it matter, if every step is taking him further from his home. His first and great need is to be turned right about ; and this turning is *conversion*, the objective phase of the change which, when considered subjectively, Scripture calls repentance ; a change, moreover, which depends upon belief of the gospel. " To the Gentiles hath God granted *repentance* unto life," we read in the Acts of the Apostles. Referring to the same event, Paul and Barnabas announced at Antioch, that " God had opened the door of *faith* unto the Gentiles " ; and elsewhere, again, it is alluded to as " the *conversion* of the Gentiles." The same event was thus described in various aspects of it ; and yet another might have been added, bringing in the fact of the new birth.

This change then, and the need of it, are indisputable realities. Whether we open the Scriptures, or turn to our own hearts, or look out upon the world around us, we find clear proofs and tokens that man's course by nature leads downwards ; that there is a controversy pending between the creature and his God. And from first to last that controversy has been the same in its nature and results ; but, as already shown, the ground and subject of it changed when the Son of God was manifested. Repentance and conversion were not less necessary in presence of a rejected Christ, than in view of a broken law ; but the whole controversy between God and man now became centred in Christ ; and therefore, acknowledging Him, believing in Him, implied, and carried with it the great change, the turning of the man to God. Hence the prominence which faith has in the gospel. The word " believe " occurs about a hundred times in the Gospel of John, and, as already stated, " repent " is not found even once. To believe in Christ involves a turning of heart to Him, and that is the only true conversion, the only true repentance.

I have mentioned the Spirit's work as another hindrance to man's efforts after salvation, and in truth it is the crowning difficulty. Faith and repentance, however they be regarded, seem to be within human capacity ; but if the Holy Ghost must act, before a sinner can have life, man falls back helplessly in presence of the sovereignty of God. And here let me say that this is precisely the value of the *doctrine* of the new birth in connection with the gospel. It is to convince man that salvation is impossible as far as human effort is concerned, and thus to cast him wholly upon God. He who preaches the Spirit's work without regard to the condition of his hearers is like a quack who, because one patient has been cured by a certain remedy, administers it promiscuously to all. " Ye must be born again " was addressed to Nicodemus, but not to the Samaritan woman at the well, nor to the multitude around the pool of Bethesda.[1] It was true, doubtless, for all, but it was not the special truth they needed ; and the

[1] John iv. and v.

more the Lord's words are weighed and studied, the more we shall be struck by the wisdom with which truth was ever ministered by Him.

In this view, indeed, the 3d, 4th, and 5th chapters of John demand the earnest and unceasing study of all who preach the gospel. In the 5th chapter, the Lord's hearers are the multitude, brought together by the miracle He has just performed, and further interested by the opposition of the Pharisees. And to such He gives a threefold testimony : first, to His own personal dignity and glory ; then, to life for the sinner through His word ; and lastly, to judgment coming upon those to whom that word does not bring life. Here we have a general testimony suited to the common need of all ; but in each of the other chapters we have special dealing with the intricacies of a special case. In the 4th chapter we are face to face with a sinner living in open immorality, yet without any sense of sin—a case more common than we are apt to think, where a sinful course is not so much the result of a depraved heart or an abandoned will, as of a conscience wholly dead. And here He seeks, first to interest, and then to awaken her, and finally He declares Himself.

But in Nicodemus we have a man who is ostensibly in the right path. His coming to Christ is itself a proof that he is a seeker after God. But he comes claiming a position that ousts grace altogether, and the Saviour must bring him to His feet before He can be a Saviour to him. Supposing himself already in the kingdom, he comes to the Lord as a God-sent Teacher ; but the Lord

" answers " him at once by declaring the need of the Spirit's work. Had the Lord exposed sin in Nicodemus, he would earnestly have repented of it. Had He unfolded to him a higher morality than he had ever learned, he would eagerly have pursued it. But, " Ye must be born again " not only put him outside the threshold within which he claimed a place, but seemed withal to shut the door against him.[1]

It is no longer now " the teacher of Israel "

---

[1] The common interpretation of John iii. 5, which connects it with " Christian baptism," not only fritters away the meaning of the passage, but involves a very glaring anachronism. It appears from the 12th verse that the doctrine related to the kingdom as known to Israel—it pertained to " earthly things." And from verse 10 we learn that the Lord's word ought to have been understood by a Jewish Rabbi ; *i.e.*, that it was truth contained in the Old Testament Scriptures. The well-taught Scribe would at once have turned to Ezekiel's prophecy, " I will sprinkle clean water upon you and ye shall be clean, . . . and I will put My spirit within you." Or if he missed the reference at first, the words that follow, " The wind bloweth where it listeth," etc., might well afford the clew to the passage on which they are so plainly based : " Come from the four winds, O breath, and breathe upon these slain that they may live " (Ezek. xxxvi. 25–27, xxxvii. 9). The " clean water " alludes of course to the rite enjoined in Num. xix. (see p. 127 *post*). Nicodemus claimed his place within the kingdom by virtue of his nationality, as Israel might have done had they been faithful. But in the carnal and apostate condition of the nation, this showed thorough ignorance not only of the things of God, but of the plain teaching of the Scriptures. No one could have any part in the kingdom without the cleansing typified by the water of purification, and the regeneration promised in Ezekiel's prophecy. The reference in the Nicodemus sermon is to that rite and to that promise, and not, I need scarcely add, to a dogma which the Church in its apostasy based upon a false interpretation of this very passage. And if without this new birth from God, the Jew, even on his high platform of privilege and covenant, could not receive his promised blessings, how doubly true must be the word to us, " Ye must be born again."

seeking wisdom from " the Teacher come from God," but the sinner in the presence of his Saviour, seeking pardon and life. The declaration of the love of God and of the lifting up of Christ, are not the answer to the difficulty, " How can these things be ? " but the answer to the need which that difficulty has awakened in the heart of Nicodemus. The mystery which Nicodemus, " the teacher of Israel," could not fathom, is solved for Nicodemus the sinner, in hearing and believing the word of Christ.

It was thus the Master preached. With the profligate Samaritan, He probed with matchless grace and wisdom the festering but hidden wound of sin. For the ignorant and needy multitude He flung the door of mercy open wide, that all might enter there. But with the Pharisee, who slighted grace, He seemed to change His purpose, and to close that door against him ; yet no sooner did he take the sinner's place than Nicodemus found the way as free and open as the power and love of God could make it. So was it again when He declared Himself to be the bread of God come down from heaven to give life unto the world. One and another may have hearkened, and to such the blessing was as full and free as grace itself. But with the rest who kicked against the word, the Lord withdrew behind the sovereignty of God, and rebuked their murmurs by the truth that no one can come to Him except the Father draw him.[1]

Here, then, is the value of the Spirit's work. For the humble penitent it bridges over and conceals

[1] John vi. 32–44.

the gulf that separates the sinner from his God. For the self-righteous or profane, it serves but to prove that gulf to be impassable. To the one it testifies of sovereign *grace*, to the other it testifies that grace is *sovereign*.[1]

The Holy Ghost has come, and now He gives a double testimony. He bears witness against the world's rejection of the Son, and He testifies to the rejected One as now exalted to be a Saviour. It is His mission to convict the world of sin, of righteousness, and of judgment : of sin, because the Son of God has been cast out by earth ; of righteousness, because the Outcast of earth has been welcomed by the Father in heaven ; and of judgment, because Satan, who put forth all his power against Him, has now himself been judged.[2] The presence of the Comforter is proof that Christ has triumphed, and a token of judgment on the world now lying in the wicked one.

But if God testifies to judgment in this day of mercy, it is in order thus to turn men's hearts to grace. And to the sinner who looks up to heaven for pardon, the mission of the Comforter is only to speak of Christ. The Spirit is come down to bear witness to the Saviour. But His is not like the Baptist's testimony, telling of a greater than

[1] I am speaking here, of course, only of the Holy Ghost in connection with the gospel testimony. His sealing and indwelling the believer, and the fruits thereof ; His baptism of all believers into the body of Christ, which is the Church of God, and the relationships and duties arising from that unity ; and His presence in that Church on earth as Christ's true and only Vicar—these are truths beyond the limits of my theme.

[2] John xvi. 8–11.

Himself to follow. His word is itself the power by which dead souls are born again to God. The love of God to man, and the cross of Christ which manifests that love, and the inspired page which contains the record of it, would all be of no avail to save a single sinner, were it not for the Spirit's work.

But men draw strange inferences here. " Preaching the Spirit's work," as it is usually understood, seems based upon the thought that the Holy Ghost has interests and claims peculiar to Himself ; and so the sinner must propitiate Him by prayer or worship in order to secure His aid. But all such thoughts are wholly false. Christianity is a great system of mediation. The Son came down to earth, not to supplant the Father, but to reveal Him ; the words He spoke were not His own, but His that sent Him. The Spirit has come down, not to supplant the Son, but to bear witness to Him. He does not speak from Himself, but receives of Christ for us. " He that hath seen Me hath seen the Father " was the word of Christ. He that has heard the Spirit's voice has received both the Father and the Son.[1] We are not regenerated in order to believe. The Word of God is itself the seed by which we are begotten.[2] Faith comes—not by prayer, for there can be no true prayer without it ;[3] nor yet by any work of the Spirit in the soul,

---

[1] John xiii. 20.   [2] I Pet. i. 23.

[3] " In maintaining the duty of praying before believing, you cannot surely be asserting that it is your duty to go to God in unbelief ? You cannot mean to say that you ought to go to God believing that He is *not* willing to bless you, in order that, by so praying, you may persuade Him to make you believe that He *is*

apart from the message which He brings—faith comes by hearing, and it is by the hearing of faith that the Spirit is received.[1]

The prayer of Philip, that Christ would reveal to him the Father,[2] was not more unintelligent and wrong than a prayer for the Spirit to reveal the Saviour. Apart from the Holy Ghost no one can be saved. Therefore He has come that no one need be lost. Christians speak too often of His work as though it were a limitation upon grace. God intends it as a crowning proof that grace is boundless and triumphant.

It is the sovereignty of God that makes the Spirit's work so insurmountable a barrier on the way to life ; but when the sinner comes to know that God's sovereignty is entirely on his side, the mountain which seemed to close heaven against him becomes a plain , nay, rather, it rises now behind him to bar the way to the City of Destruction.

It may be important that the theologian should define these truths ; but the work of the preacher is to set forth Christ, and it is thus alone that the need of the true hearer can be met. The burdened sinner who came face to face with Him in the streets of Jerusalem or the village ways of Galilee, and

willing. Are you to persist in unbelief till in some miraculous way faith drops into you, and God compels you to believe ?

" Understanding prayer in the scriptural sense, I would tell every man to *pray*, just as I would tell every man to *believe* ; for prayer includes and presupposes faith. ' Whosoever shall call on the name of the Lord shall be saved.' But then the apostle adds, ' How shall they call on Him in whom they have not believed.' " (Dr. H. Bonar's *God's Way of Peace*.)

The logic of Rom. x. 13, 14, is absolutely inexorable on this point.

[1] Gal. iii 2   [2] John xiv. 8.

heard words that revealed to him the Christ of God, received, with the revelation, peace and life and the birthright of heaven. He might have been unable to explain faith or to define repentance,[1] and ignorant of the doctrine of the Spirit ; but yet he had repented, and believed, and been born again. And the blessing is as near to men now as in the days of the Lord's humiliation, and the way of life is just the same. There is blessing for the sinner as freely, and on the same ground. If then some reader of these pages should be kept from Christ by misgivings based on false thoughts of repentance or the Spirit's work, let him turn away to Him who now speaks from heaven the words which once He uttered upon earth, and, hearing and believing, receive the blessing which the testimony brings : " Verily, verily, I say unto you, he that heareth My word and believeth on Him that sent Me, hath everlasting life, and shall not come into judgment, but is passed from death into life " (John v. 24).

THE PRODIGAL'S RETURN

I think upon the past, and feel
My heart sink hopelessly, and fears
Of judgment seize on me ; I kneel
Before my God, and own that years

---

[1] I know no definition of repentance equal to that of the Westminster Divines (*Shorter Catechism*, Q. 87). But when men begin by confounding conviction with contrition, and go on to insist upon a certain amount of it as a condition precedent to receiving blessing, it is sheer error. Moreover, it is wholly untrue that the convert must be subjectively conscious of the various elements of the change involved in repentance, or even doctrinally acquainted with them. The qualities of the new nature may be latent for a time ; and in the deepest repentance, all thought of self and sin may be lost in the overwhelming appreciation of present grace.

And years of deep, dark, deadly guilt
  Are dragging down my soul to hell.
I know the wretched hopes I've built
  Of heaven, if His judgment fell
On me, would vanish as a dream :
  Before the dreadful judgment throne,
Such hopes, I know, though they may seem
  All fair and right, when by our own
Poor godless hearts surveyed, would all
  But serve to prove what godless hearts
We had, to cling to them at all.
  O God, my life no hope imparts,
And yet I scarcely dare to hope
  In Thee. My heart is like a stone ;
My soul is dead ; I blindly grope,
  And long for light. And yet I own
It is not Thee, but only rest
  And safety for my soul, I seek,
My guilty soul. O God, at best
  I'm godless, even while I speak
To Thee ! Not love but selfish fear
  It is that brings me to Thy feet ;
My wretched sins are far more dear
  To me—but then, Thy judgment-seat !
Ah ! yes, I own, were there no hell,
  I would not seek Thy heaven, O God ;
A Father's love is not the spell
  That draws me, but Thy judgment rod.

O God, I cannot ask for bread,
  For bread, I know, is children's fare,
And I'm a dog ; [1] I bow my head,
  And own I'm but a dog : nor dare
I seek to claim a higher place ;
  I have no right to children's meat ;
I only cast myself on grace,
  I lay me prostrate at Thy feet.
O God, have mercy on my soul :
  Before th' eternal night begins,
O save my dark and guilty soul ;
  Forgive my sins—O God, my sins !

---

[1] Matt. xv. 26.

Hast Thou not given Thine only Son
  To bear my sins upon the tree ?
And wilt Thou now, when all is done,
  Refuse, my God, to pardon me ?
And, O my God, hast Thou not said,
  " He that believeth on the Son
Hath life " ? and I believe ; though red
  Like crimson are my sins, and one
By one they rise before me now,
  Sins long forgotten, and they fain
Would make me doubt Thy word : I bow
  My head in shame : yet wilt Thou deign
To look on me ? If I am lost,
  I need a Saviour : 'tis for such
He came to die ; and what a cost
  To pay ! 'tis not for me to touch
That finished work of His, or seek
  To add a sigh, or tear, or groan
Of mine to what He bore, or speak
  Of aught in me but sin. Alone,
O Christ, Thou hadst to bear my doom
  To take my deep dark curse on Thee,
And bear it all ; and now there's room
  For grace to pardon even me.

Then look on me, my Father. Yes,
  I call Thee Father, for I know
Thy word is sure, and humbly bless
  The grace that deigned to stoop so low,
That such as I can come to Thee,
  And as a sinner reconciled
By His most precious blood, for me
  Once shed, can know that I'm Thy child.

'Tis but a moment since I thought
  There scarce was hope for one like me ;
I heeded not the love that bought
  Me with the blood of Calvary.
Yet now I dare to look above
  And call Thee Father ; though my heart's
Defiled, my lips unclean—Thy love
  Has conquered fear—though Satan's darts

Fall thick around me, and within
  I dare not look—'tis like a sea
That cannot rest, and full of sin—
  I now can look away to Thee,
And find in Thee my peace, nor fear
  To rest my trembling sin-stained soul
Upon Thy word, and so draw near.
  My Saviour's blood has made me whole.
I'm black and worthless, but I'm Thine ;
  My God I'm Thine ; to Thee I owe
My life, my life to Thee resign.
  O teach Thy child in life to show
Thy praises forth. I bless Thy name ;
  I worship, magnify, adore,
And praise Thy great and glorious name ,
  O fill my soul yet more and more
With praise to Thee. The " miry clay " [1]
  Still clings to me, and yet I raise
My triumph song and bless the day :
  O fill my soul yet more with praise !

---

[1] Ps. xl. 2.

6

ELECTION

WHEN the gift of life was proffered us, we were conscious in accepting it that we did so freely, voluntarily. Since then, we have come to see that grace did not exhaust itself even in working out our deliverance at a cost so priceless, and bringing it within our reach, but that our very acceptance of the gift was the Spirit's work, and as directly the action of grace as Calvary itself. But more than this, now that we have received the message, and are come within the scene of joy and blessing to which it bids us, we have to learn that, in a sense deeper and fuller still, grace is sovereign. The gospel of our salvation spanned the open door of grace as we approached it ; above the inner portal, we now read the words " Chosen in Him before the foundation of the world."

And surely this mystery of election is both fitted and intended to bring deep blessing to the believing heart ; but the sad fact is too patent to be ignored, that with the vast majority of Christians it is so inseparably linked with controversy as to be removed from blessing altogether. Upon one side, the plain testimony of Scripture is tampered with, if not rejected ; upon the other, the doctrine is asserted with a narrowness which is uncongenial, if not absolutely incompatible with truth.

To introduce into these pages a treatise upon the election controversy would be obviously a departure from their plan and purpose. I will content myself, therefore, with offering a few remarks in passing, for the consideration of the thoughtful reader. First, the scriptural expression " God's elect," is not the mere statement of a fact, or even of a purpose, but, like " first-born," [1] it is a title of dignity and privilege, applicable exclusively to the Christian. And secondly, the prominent thought in election, especially in this dispensation of the *Church* (as the very word *ecclesia* suggests), is rank and privilege, not deliverance from perdition.[2] The distinctive truth of election must not be lost in the kindred but wider truth of the sovereignty of God.

And if a full exposition of election would here be out of place, still more so would be a defence of it. It needs not to be defended, for it is plainly taught in Scripture.[3] But the theological doctrine based upon it is too often pressed beyond the limits of the positive teaching of Holy Writ, and thus the divine mystery which crowns the great truth of sovereign grace, is degraded to the level of a narrow dogma, inconsistent alike with both sovereignty and grace.

[1] Heb. xii. 23.

[2] A cogent proof of both these statements is afforded by the fact, that the title of " elect," like that of " first-born," primarily applies to Christ Himself. (1 Pet. ii. 4, 6 ; Luke xxiii. 35.)

[3] One passage may suffice—" We are bound to give thanks alway to God for you, brethren beloved of the Lord, because God hath from the beginning chosen you to salvation through sanctification of the Spirit and belief of the truth ; whereunto He called you by our gospel." (2 Thess. ii. 13, 14).

I desire therefore to treat the subject only as it bears upon my theme, and to show that election cannot either warp or limit the plain meaning of the gracious words in which the gospel message comes to us.

One of the most popular systems of metaphysics is based upon the fact that certain of our ideas seem to spring from the essential constitution of the mind itself ; and these are not subject to our reason, but, on the contrary, they control it. A superficial thinker might suppose the powers of human imagination to be boundless. He can imagine the sun and moon and stars to disappear from the heavens, and the peopled earth to vanish from beneath his feet, leaving him a solitary unit in boundless space ; but let him try, pursuing still further his madman's dream, to grasp the thought of space itself being annihilated, and his mind, in obedience to some inexorable law, will refuse the conception altogether. Or, to take an illustration apter for my present purpose, wild fancy may thus change the universe into a blank, but, though there should remain no shadow and no dial, no sequence of events, the mind is utterly incapable of imagining how time could cease to flow. And the practical conclusion we arrive at is that our idea of " past, present, and future," like that of space, is not derived from experience, but depends upon a law imposed upon our reason by the God who made us.

I am far from appealing to German philosophy in defence of God's truth, but I do enthusiastically appeal to it as a protest against the arrogance of limiting God by the standard of our own ignorance and frailty. What is, in plain words, the practical difficulty of election in its bearing upon the gospel ? Why, that at some epoch in the past, God decided that this or that individual was to be saved or lost ; and, therefore, that his future depends, not on the present action of the grace or the righteousness of the living God Who can appeal through the gospel to his heart and conscience, but on what is nothing more or less than an iron decree of fate. May not the whole difficulty depend on the arrogant supposition that God Himself is bound by the same laws that He has imposed upon His creatures ? [1]

But whatever we may think of the theories of Kant, this at least is certain, that there is no deception in the gospel as proclaimed by God to men. " Truth is one " ; and though, to our finite minds, election and grace may seem as far as the poles asunder, and as antagonistic as the magnetic currents which set toward them ; to the Infinite they may appear but inseparable parts of one great whole. Every truth has its own place ; and there is no more reason why grace should be denied by dragging election into the gospel, than why election should be denied, because, when so thrust out of its proper sphere, it seems to be opposed to grace. " Rightly dividing the Word of truth," is a precept which we need to remember here.

I repeat, there is no deception in the gospel. Some men who can preach with freedom to a multitude, are very often puzzled when face to face with an individual : the heart and the head are at issue directly, and they either throw their

[1] See in passing Ps. xc. 4, and 2 Pet. iii. 8.

theology overboard, and preach grace boldly, or else they state the gospel so ingeniously that the difficulty created by their views about election is kept out of sight. In the gospel of God there is no reservation whatsoever. And let us remember that it is *His* gospel, " *God's good news* concerning His Son Jesus Christ our Lord." [1] Mark also that it is not " concerning the sinner." To some the distinction may appear self-evident, and to others it may seem so trifling as almost to savour of a quibble ; but in fact it is at the root of many of our difficulties and mistakes in gospel preaching. The gospel then is God's good news about Christ. And this gospel is as true for a single individual as for a crowd ; and, moreover, it is absolutely and unequivocally true whether men believe it or not.

Another most important practical distinction is that the gospel is, strictly speaking, not a doctrinal statement, but a divine proclamation. " Believe on the Lord Jesus Christ and thou shalt be saved " was Paul's answer to the question of the jailer at Philippi, to explain to him that salvation was on the principle, not of doing, but of faith in Christ. The next verse adds, " and they spake to him the word of the Lord " ; that is, they preached the gospel to him.[2] Now some preachers, instead of proclaiming the gospel, appeal unceasingly to their hearers to believe in Christ ; and the consequence is too often that, instead of having their thoughts turned to the person and work of the Saviour, people are occupied with efforts to get faith. And the difficulty is frequently increased by

[1] Rom. i. 1–3.   [2] Acts xvi. 30–32.

reading the second chapter of Ephesians as though " the gift of God " there spoken of were *faith*.[1] *Salvation* is the gift of God : " *faith* cometh by hearing, and hearing by the Word of God."

But the distinctions I have noticed, important though they be, serve only to clear the ground for the consideration of the real question here raised— How can grace be compatible with election ? The gospel proclaims universal reconciliation,[2] and grace is " salvation-bringing to all men."[3] Election, on the other hand, assumes that the believer's blessings are the result of a divine decree. These, it is objected, are wholly inconsistent, and one or other of them must be explained away. Doubtless they may appear to be incompatible, but to maintain that therefore they are so in fact, is to put reason above revelation, or in other words, to place man above God. Is the Christian to reject truths so plainly taught, because, forsooth, they are beset with difficulties of a kind which even German metaphysics would suffice to solve ! [4]

Nor are the difficulties here involved at all

---

[1] Eph. ii. 8, see note, p. 54 *ante*.   [2] See chap. x. *post*.

[3] Not in fact, but in intention ; in its scope and purpose it is σωτήριος πᾶσιν ἀνθρώποις. Tit. ii. 11.

[4] True it is that what is clearly contrary to reason must be rejected ; but so far from what is here contended for being against reason, it is perfectly consistent with a recognised system of metaphysics, than which, moreover, when separated from the jargon of a certain school, none is more philosophical. This then is the object of my appeal to Kant. I should deprecate the pedantry of introducing a discussion of the critical philosophy in such a connection, and I do not pretend that it affords the true solution of the seeming paradox of election and grace ; *I notice it merely to show how easily the difficulty may be solved.* Surely the Christian may be content to accept the mystery, and to trust God for the solution of it.

peculiar to the present question. The very same objection which many Christians urge against the gospel, is used by the infidel to prove the absurdity of prayer. Will the great God, " with whom is no variableness, neither shadow of turning," change His purpose at the cry of a sinful creature ? A man once " prayed earnestly that it might not rain, and it rained not on the earth by the space of three years and six months ; and he prayed again, and the heavens gave rain, and the earth brought forth her fruit." [1] Nor can we tolerate the figment that the prayer itself was but another result of the inexorable rule of fate. We do not trust in fate, but in " the *living* God," and we are taught the solemnity and reality of prayer, not merely by the record of the blessings it has won, but by the ominous words, " He gave them their own desire," [2] endorsed on many a rebellious cry sent up to heaven by His people.

But there is another prayer, of which the solemn record should suffice to set at rest every doubt that a perverted use of the doctrine of election has cast upon the truth of grace. The Lord Himself, though come down to earth that He might drink the cup which brimmed over upon Calvary, could pray, upon the very eve of Calvary, that that cup might pass from Him. He, " the Lamb slain from the foundation of the world "—He, who, ere a few days had passed, could chide His doubting disciples with the word " Ought not Christ to have suffered these things ? " recapitulating in their wondering ears the oft-told record of prophecy

[1] Jas. v. 17, 18.　　　　[2] Ps. lxxviii. 29.

which Calvary fulfilled—*He* found, neither in that record, nor in the divine purpose it unfolded, anything to hinder the prayer of Gethsemane, " O My Father, if it be possible, let this cup pass from Me." [1] With Him the dire necessity to drink it arose from no stern and irrevocable edict of the past, but from the sovereign will of a present living God, Who, even then, would hearken to His cry if redemption could be won at any price less terrible and costly ; [2] and yet there are some who would rebuke a Christian mother for pouring out her heart in prayer, without reserve or fear, that God would save the children He has given her ! [3]

Eternity is God's domain, but no less is " the living present " in His hand, and if the doctrine of election become a limitation of His power to bless and save, it degenerates into a denial of the very truth on which it rests—the sovereignty of Jehovah.

The plausible but empty objection may perchance be urged, that the relations between the Father and the incarnate Son, are so different from those which govern His dealings with sinful men, that the inference here drawn from the record of Gethsemane is worthless. I will therefore press

[1] Matt. xxvi. 39.

[2] Or if the Lord were pleased unconditionally to claim deliverance. (See Matt. xxvi. 53.)

[3] Among the strange phenomena of practical Christian life, one of the saddest is that so often witnessed of Christian parents attributing to a divine decree the fact of their children growing up unconverted. " Having *believing* children " was one of the qualifications of a bishop, because it was a pledge and proof of the parents' faithfulness to God. (Tit. i. 6.) The precept " Bring them up in the nurture and admonition of the Lord," implies a promise ; and God's implicit promises are sure and certain.

the matter further, and call attention to the fact
that this paradox of election and grace, so far
from being in any sense without a parallel, is merely
a single phase of the great mystery of divine
sovereignty in relation to human will. A passage
in Peter's Pentecostal sermon may be cited to
illustrate my meaning : " Him, being delivered by
the determinate counsel and foreknowledge of
God, ye have taken, and by wicked hands have
crucified and slain." [1] The murderers of Christ
were acting in fulfilment of a divine decree, and
yet their deeds were really and absolutely their
own. Theirs were "*wicked* hands," and guilt of
necessity supposes the action of an independent
will. When this can be explained, that they who
set up the cross on Calvary were fulfilling a divine
purpose, though acting in direct antagonism to
the divine will, the clew will have been found to
every difficulty here alluded to.

Nor is this mystery peculiar to great and
momentous events foretold in prophecy ; it sur-
rounds our life from first to last. To recognise
and act upon the fact of our own responsibility and
freedom, and yet to accept the consequences of
our acts as coming from the hand of God, is the
part of a spiritual Christian. But to act upon the
truth of divine sovereignty, yielding to blind im-
pulse as guiding the execution of its decrees, is the
part of a heathen fatalist. As I leave my door, I
am conscious of being absolutely free to turn to
the right hand or to the left. The one path may
lead to the attainment of some signal blessing, the

[1] Acts ii. 23.

other to the commission of some terrible sin : I make choice, and in choosing the wrong path I am sensible, not only that I have power to take the other, but that I am going in direct violation of the will of God in not taking it. When the consequences are startling, as for instance if my error cost me my life, every one recognises the sovereignty of God in the whole matter, but that truth applies as really to the fall of a sparrow as to the death of a king.[1] And thus every day of our lives we *act* upon a principle which appears to be absolutely incompatible with sovereignty ; and yet we recognise this truth of sovereignty in reviewing our actions and their consequences.

And so it is precisely with the true evangelist. He goes forth with a proclamation which *seems* to ignore election, as the full gospel revealed to the Apostle of the Gentiles always does ;[2] but, as he reviews his labours, his thought is " As many as were ordained to eternal life believed." [3]

If the truth of election hinders or even shapes his testimony, it is proof that he has yet to learn the truth of grace. Sin reigned once. God was dealing with men on the ground of their being what they ought to be, while by their very nature they were what they ought not to be. God's attitude toward the sinner therefore was adverse. There was a

---

[1] Matt. x. 29.

[2] " My gospel," Rom. xvi. 25, and see also 1 Tim. i. 11.

[3] Acts xiii. 48. Those who are zealous for the truth of election always lay emphasis upon these words ; but they ignore the words which follow : " *they so spake* that a great multitude believed " (xiv. 1). This phrase οὕτως ὥστε occurs again only in John iii. 16,

covenant no doubt, but that only served to make the doom of the world more definite. God was imputing sin, and the normal and legitimate result to men was death. But now sin is dethroned, and grace is reigning. God is no longer imputing sin, but preaching peace. He to whom all judgment is committed [1] is now seated on a throne of grace. It is not that He has grace for the elect and judgment for all besides, but that grace is the great characteristic of His reign. He is a Saviour, and not a Judge.[2] He shall yet come to judge ; but now, the amnesty has been proclaimed, and judgment waits. It is not, as in a bygone dispensation, that there is mercy for a favoured class, but that there is mercy, and nothing else, for all without distinction. The day is coming when judgment will be as unmixed as grace is now, but during all this " acceptable year of the Lord," His throne is a throne of grace, and the guiltiest sinner upon earth will find there only mercy.

And *this* is " the good news of the grace of God." [3] Election can in no way limit it. To raise the question whether unconverted men around us are elect, is to betray ignorance both of election and of grace. " Secret things belong unto the Lord," and it is not ours to attempt to fathom the deep mysteries of that death on Calvary ; but this at least is plain as the noonday sun, that that death has in such sense settled the question of sin, that sin is no longer a barrier between the sinner and his God.[4] The sin is still upon his head, and judgment will overwhelm

---

[1] John v. 22. [2] John xii. 47. [3] Acts xx. 24.
[4] *Judicially* I mean. *Morally*, sin must always separate from God.

him if he die unsaved ; but it is none the less true that the death of Christ has made it a righteous thing in God to proclaim Himself a Saviour, and to preach pardon and peace to every creature.

There is no shuffling of the cards ; there is no deception in it. If forgiveness is preached to all, it is because all may share it. If God beseeches men to be reconciled, it is because He has provided a reconciliation ; if He appeals to them to come to Him, it is because the way is open right up to His throne and to His heart. It is impossible that election can ever limit the value of the death of Christ, or the power of that mighty name to save and bless. Sovereignty ! Why, the universe will have no such proof of the depth of His counsels and the almightiness of His power, as that of heaven filled with sinners saved from hell.

With some the difficulty springs from treating the gospel as though it were a problem as to the amount of suffering endured by Christ, and the numerical quantity of the sins atoned for. But God points us to the cross with a far different object ; and the power of the gospel is to know what it is to *Him*. It is Himself that God would present before the sinner, and He points to that cross in proof of the vastness of the sacrifice, and the boundlessness of the love that made it. He so loved the world that He gave His only-begotten Son —and He adds, not as a cold formula which the initiated know to be overshadowed by the doctrine of election, but as the expression of the longing of that mighty love—" that WHOSOEVER believeth in Him should not perish but have everlasting life."

7

SUBSTITUTION

In the days so lately passed away, when debt was treated as a crime, we can imagine how a dishonest and vindictive creditor may have received satisfaction of his claim without his debtor's knowledge, and have kept him still in prison for the debt. If in some strange combination of circumstances such an event occurred, great must have been the indignation of all good men against him who traded upon his debtor's ignorance to hold him still liable for a debt which was in fact discharged.

And thousands there are of earnest people in whose minds the story of redemption seems to put God in the place of the dishonest creditor. If that death on Calvary be indeed the payment of His people's debt, how can forgiveness now be preached as being of grace ? Is it not a matter of the strictest justice, that they whose discharge was nailed to the cross of Christ nineteen centuries ago, should, at the earliest moment possible, be set free ? How can it be honest, or true, or right, to urge men to flee from the wrath to come, seeing that for some all wrath has been already borne, and the infliction of it now would be an outrage upon justice, and that for the rest there is no refuge open ? Is not the proclamation of the gospel like holding forth to the sinner the account of God's outstanding claims against him, with the assurance that the hand of the great Creditor is ready to sign his discharge for ever, the moment he repents ? And does not every principle of truth and right forbid that the elect should be scared into repentance by concealment of the fact that the ink upon their discharge was dry long centuries ago, and that others should be tantalised with deceptive promises of blessings they can never know, enforced by threats of judgment from which, for them, there is no escape ?

For those who either ignore the great truth of divine righteousness in connection with our salvation, or fritter away the revelation of divine love to a lost world, such questions as these will only provoke a supercilious smile. But with such as have in any measure grasped the great twin truths which characterise Christianity, a juster estimate will be formed of these perplexities, and a worthier value set upon any honest effort toward the solution of them. It will therefore be here my aim to show that all such difficulties spring, not from the gospel itself, nor from the teaching of Holy Writ, but solely from forms of expression, and modes of thought, about the death of Christ, which are unwarranted by Scripture. And this end will perhaps be best attained by offering first a positive statement of the truth upon this subject, as it is unfolded in the types of the Old Testament and in the doctrinal teaching of the New.

Redemption is presented to us in the Scriptures

in a twofold aspect, as connected both with *power* and with *blood*. Israel was redeemed out of Egypt —redeemed " with an outstretched arm." [1] In another sense Israel was redeemed *in* Egypt by the blood of the paschal lamb. But it is essential to remember that the redemption of the people was complete ere ever they commenced their wilderness journey. It depended, therefore, not upon the offerings of the law, but upon the passover in Egypt. The rites enjoined in Leviticus were for a redeemed and holy people ; it was by the sacrifices recorded in Exodus that Israel attained that privileged position. It is specially to Exodus, therefore, that we must turn to learn the truth of the death of Christ in its aspect toward the unsaved.

I say this without wishing in the least to pander to the tendency that prevails to map out the Scriptures by hard-and-fast lines like the squares of a chess-board. The Word of God is a two-edged sword, with a side both for saved and unsaved ; but the secret of attaining clear and scriptural thoughts is to seek first the primary application of every truth or text, and then, without danger of error or confusion, we can apply it in the widest sense. Israel's title to the benefits of the sin offerings depended on the passover ; [2] let us then mark the difference between the two.

In the case of the sin-offerings, the offerer came to the door of the tabernacle to give his life as the

---

[1] Ex. vi. 6 ; Deut. vii. 8.

[2] As regards the distinctions hereinafter pointed out, the dedication offering of the covenant (Ex. xxiv.) was in the same category with the passover.

penalty for his sin, and there, having identified the victim with himself by laying his hand upon its head, the death of the sacrifice was accepted instead of his own.[1] And this is what we understand by *substitution* ; the sinner laid his sin upon the animal, and the victim died instead of him. And here the *death* was everything. Whatever ceremonial followed was the care of the priest, and not of the offerer ; that is, of God, and not of the sinner. But, as we have seen, this was a provision for a people already redeemed. Israel's right to the services of the priest depended on redemption accomplished.[2]

But with the great redemption sacrifice of the passover it was wholly different. The dread death-sentence had gone out against all the land of Egypt. None were excepted from it. It embraced alike king and captive, Hebrew and Egyptian. But for Israel that sentence was fulfilled in the blood of the paschal lamb. But how ? There was no laying of the hand upon the head of the victim, as with the sin-offerings. The death of the lamb, though doubtless the foundation of every blessing, would in itself have brought no deliverance. Beyond the threshold of the blood-stained door, the Israelite would have shared in Egypt's doom ; beneath the shelter of that blood, the Egyptian would have shared in Israel's redemption. The death upon which their deliverance depended was accomplished ; but their participation in the benefits of that death depended entirely upon the sprinkling of the victim's blood. There was no question

[1] Lev. iv. 4, 15, 24, 29 ; 2 Chron. xxix. 23, etc.
[2] This point is fully treated of in chap. ix. *post.*

of substitution, in the sense of the sin-offering. The benefits of the sin-offering were secured to him whose hand had rested on the victim's head, and they could neither be extended nor transferred. And so also with the great day of atonement ; it was only for Israel.[1]

It was the same great sacrifice, doubtless, which all these types prefigured for Israel and illustrate for us, but in different aspects of it. And the way to follow aright the teaching of the types is to regard their historical sequence as marking their moral order. We thus learn the different aspects of the death of Christ, and the divine order of the truth concerning it. I have contrasted the types of Exodus with the offerings of the law ; but there is one rite of Leviticus which presents all this truth at a single view, marking the moral order above distinguished. I allude to the cleansing of the leper.[2] The leper's birds are the correlative of no offering of the law, but of the Exodus sacrifices. Then followed the trespass-offering, the sin-offering, and the burnt-offering with its meat-offering. I will here speak only of the birds and the sin-offering. According to the analogy of the great day of atonement, the twofold aspect of the same offering is presented by *two* victims, the one being killed, the other sent out of sight. But mark here the same distinction as that already noticed between the sin-offering and the passover. The leper's identification with the

---

[1] The stranger might eat the passover and share in the offerings, if brought within the covenant by circumcision. (Ex. xii. 48; Num. ix. 14, xv. 26–29.)

[2] Lev. xiv., and see note p. 32 *ante*.

victim's death depended on his being sprinkled with its blood; but when he came to offer his sin-offering he identified the victim with himself beforehand.[1]

In respect of both, the death accomplished was *for* the leper, but in senses wholly different. The one blood-shedding was, as with the passover, a means by which deliverance might be gained, but until that blood was sprinkled the sinner had no part in it. The other was a substitutional sacrifice, and the result to the offerer depended immediately, and only, upon the victim's death. In both cases the death was *for* the unclean person; but in the latter it was *instead* of him.

These different aspects of the death of Christ, though carefully distinguished in Scripture, are hopelessly confounded in theology; and that confusion has given rise to the difficulties now under consideration, and others of a kindred nature. " Bearing sin " is a figurative expression, and the figure is derived from the sin-offering; substitution is essentially characteristic of it. But Scripture never speaks of the death of Christ in its relation to the unbeliever—the unsaved—in language borrowed from the sin-offering.[2] Contrast the words of 1 Peter ii. 24 with Paul's sermons to the idolaters of Athens, and to the Jews of Pisidian Antioch,[3] and my meaning will be plainly seen.

---

[1] Compare Lev. iv. 29.

[2] There is one verse in the New Testament which may seem to be an exception to this (John i. 29), but I will not stop to discuss it here. I am content to refer to Dean Alford's exposition of the words : they were meant to indicate the Nazarene as being the Messiah of Isa. liii.

[3] Acts xiii. 16–41 ; xvii. 22–31.

The sermons were addressed to the unsaved ; the Epistle is for those who " have returned unto the Shepherd and Bishop of their souls." Just as with the leper's sparrow the *death* of the victim was *typically* the righteous ground on which God could pronounce him clean, but that death was nothing to him until he had been sprinkled with the blood, and then, and not till then, he was entitled to bring the sin-offering ; so the death of Christ is the righteous ground on which God can cleanse the guiltiest and vilest, and proclaim forgiveness far and near, but until the gospel is received—for faith answers to the blood sprinkling of the type—that death, though none the less precious to God, brings no pardon to the sinner.

When thus identified with the sacrifice of Calvary, but only then, the sinner may adopt the language of the sin-offering, and say " He His own self bare my sins in His own body on the tree." As the utterance of faith, such words as these are absolutely and unequivocally true ; but as a doctrinal assertion upon the lips of the unconverted, they are utterly false, and the falsehood is all the more dangerous because of the perverted truth it seems to embrace. The work of Christ has a great and real aspect to the world, but to assert this truth of substitution of the unconverted is to pander to the false peace which is ensnaring tens of thousands around us, and at the same time to sap the foundations of the Christian's faith. If the 53rd chapter of Isaiah be true of one who may yet be lost, the ground of the believer's confidence is gone , what seemed a rock beneath his feet is no better than shifting sand.

But some, perhaps, will struggle to escape from this inevitable conclusion by the strange and subtle subterfuge that, though the gospel is to be proclaimed to all, it is true only for the believer. This error is not more wicked than it is silly. If it be true only for the believer, it is false for all the rest ; and does a good and righteous God hold men guilty for refusing what is false ? The thought is sheer blasphemy. " The gospel of the glory of the blessed God " is wholly and absolutely true to all, and for all, whether they believe it or reject it—a proclamation and an appeal from sovereign grace, now free in virtue of Calvary to bless without distinction or restriction, and leaving, if unheeded or despised, the certainty of judgment. The word comes forth from an open heaven, and if, even as he turns away from Christ, the sinner could look right up to the very throne and heart of God, he would see a throne of grace, and the heart that gave the Only-begotten Son. When Jerusalem rejected the glad tidings, they who were behind the scenes could testify that there was neither reserve nor artifice in the proclamation ; and if that guilty people could have witnessed what these were privileged to behold, they would have seen a mighty Saviour pouring forth His heart in tears because their unbelief had paralysed the hand stretched forth for their deliverance.[1]

But, it will be urged, if Christ did not die as our substitute, salvation is impossible ; and if He did

[1] Luke xix. 41.

so die for us, this fact must date from **Calvary**, and not from our conversion. This assumes that the death of Christ was *instead of* some, in such a sense as to make their salvation forensically a necessity, and that the salvation of any besides is a moral impossibility. Such difficulties only prove the danger of departing from the strict accuracy of scriptural expressions in dealing with these truths. To speak of Christ's dying *instead of* us, or as our *substitute*, is to adopt the language of theology, not of Scripture, and we must take care lest we use the words in a sense or a connection inconsistent with the truth.[1] The teaching of Scripture is that He died for sinners (there is no emphasis on the preposition), and that, on believing, they become identified with Him in that death.

Let the reader turn, for example, to Peter's sermon to the household of Cornelius, and mark the character of the testimony given, ending with these

[1] The language of ancient Greece is far richer than our own in prepositions, and "*instead of*" has its unequivocal correlative ; but this word, though freely used by the LXX. (ἀντὶ : see *ex. gr.* Gen. xxx. 2, and xliv. 33), and found in the New Testament (*ex. gr.* Matt. ii. 22), is never employed in such passages as Rom. v. 6, 7, 8. The statement of Matt. xx. 28, repeated in Mark x. 45, will not be considered an exception to this by any one who marks the form and purpose of the text. The word ὑπέρ no doubt *may* have the same force, just as "*for*" in English. But in either case such a meaning is exceptional and forced ; and in our own language we should in that case pronounce the word with emphasis, and print it in italics. A full and careful consideration of every passage where the word occurs will satisfy the student that it is never so used in the New Testament. The only text in which our translators have thus rendered it (2 Cor. v. 20) is a signal proof of this. An ambassador speaks *on behalf of*, not in the stead of, the court which accredits him. I need not say that *substitution* is an extra-scriptural expression.

words :—" To Him give all the prophets witness, that through His name whosoever believeth in Him shall receive remission of sins." [1] Christ was presented, not in identification with the sinner, but objectively to faith ; and the word was added, " Whosoever believeth in Him shall receive remission of sins." The hearers believed the testimony, and then and there they were baptized with the Holy Ghost. [2] Then and not till then, the doctrine of the 6th chapter of Romans became true of them : —" We who died to sin, how shall we any longer live therein ? " [3] If Christ died as our substitute, then we ourselves are deemed to have died to sin. Of whom is this true ? The next verse gives the answer in unmistakable terms : " Or are ye ignorant that all we who were baptized into Christ Jesus [4] were baptized into His death ? " And so on through the passage, which claims careful study throughout, ending thus at the 10th and 11th verses :—" For the death which He died He died unto sin once for all, but the life which He liveth He liveth unto God. Thus do ye also account yourselves dead indeed unto sin, but alive unto God in Christ Jesus." Words could not be plainer ; all that Christ accomplished for us we, as believers, are to reckon actually true of ourselves. In the face of this chapter, to maintain that substitution is a truth for the unsaved is either playing upon words or trifling with truth. [5]

[1] Acts x. 34–43.   [2] Acts x. 44.   [3] Rom. vi. 2, R.V.
[4] Compare Acts x. 44, and 1 Cor. xii. 13.
[5] But it will be asked, are not the closing verses of 2 Cor. v. addressed to the unconverted, and do not they teach substitution ? To this question I give an emphatic negative. In common with all

Here then is the key to the difficulties stated in the opening paragraphs of the chapter. Theology with its subtleties has given rise to questions from which the simplicity of Scripture is entirely free. When the sinner believes in Christ he becomes so thoroughly identified with Him in all His vicarious work, that he can speak of Calvary as though the crucifixion were but yesterday, and he had there and then been justified thereby. But to speak of the death of Christ as having this substitutional relationship to the sinner, apart from the change

the rest of the Epistle, these verses were written to " the Church of God at Corinth with all the saints in all Achaia." In the last two verses of chapter v. and the 1st verse of chapter vi. the apostle states the character and purpose of his ministry. But the " Received Text," by interpolating " *for* " at the beginning of verse 21, and separating it from what follows, destroys the connection of the passage ; and the English Version, by introducing pronouns and altering the emphasis of the words, has utterly disguised its purpose. " On Christ's behalf, then, we are ambassadors : as though God were exhorting by us, we beseech on Christ's behalf, Be reconciled to God. Him who knew not sin He made to be sin on our behalf that we might become the righteousness of· God in Him. And [δὲ] as fellow-workers (with God) we also exhort that you receive not the grace of God to no purpose." " Our entreaty to the world is, 'Be reconciled'; to you who have received this grace our exhortation is, 'Receive it not in vain.' In our ministry to the world we are ambassadors ; in our ministry to you we are His fellow-workers." The 20th verse is in immediate connection with the 18th and 19th verses, and the last verse is introductory to the opening words of the 6th chapter, all being bracketed together as descriptive of the apostle's ministry. And the prominent thought in the passage is not the identification of the sinner with Christ, but the purpose of God to usward in making Him to be sin : it was " in order that we might become the righteousness of God in Him." It is not that He took this place *instead of us* (which, indeed, would have no meaning), and that we thereby stood free , but that He became what we were in order that we might become what He is.

which takes place on his believing; and thus to make his pardon appear to be an act of justice in such a sense that it ceases to be an act of grace, is wholly unwarranted and false. If there be those on earth whose case is beyond the scope of the work of Christ, it is not in the power of God to save them ; and thus redemption has failed of its first and highest aim, which is not the saving of the sinner, merely, but the restoring to God His sovereignty compromised by sin. But if the death of Christ be substitutionally instead of the unbeliever, his conversion may alter his condition spiritually and morally, but it can in no wise affect his judicial state : he is saved in fact and of right, whether he believes or not. *In either case, grace is in chains, and not enthroned.*[1]

There is absolutely no limit to the value of the death of Christ to Godward ; and there is not between the poles a single child of Adam who may not know its power, and receive the reconciliation

---

[1] Any who will, dismissing prejudice, compare the language of Scripture with words and phrases popular among us, will be surprised to find how much there is which is unwarranted, even in what God seems to sanction by His blessing. We must not forget, however, that grace marks all His dealings with us, and we ought therefore to be the more careful and earnest to test our words and thoughts about Christ by Holy Writ. To make apparent success the test of what is right is just as immoral in the things of God as in the affairs of men.

If any should oppose what is here urged by argument or inference, it would be an easy task to silence them with their own weapons. The imputation of sin and righteousness as taught in Scripture is reasonable in the highest sense ; but the doctrine here objected to might easily be shown to be not only false but absurd. This, however, is not the place to enter on a discussion of such a character.

which it wrought. And on the ground of this accomplished reconciliation, forgiveness is proclaimed to all without reserve or equivocation. But it is only the " *all that believe* " who are justified; [1] and if it be demanded, why, beneath the supremacy of boundless love and almighty power, the few, and not the many should be saved, we can but fall back upon divine sovereignty, and exclaim, " O the depth of the riches both of the wisdom and knowledge of God ! how unsearchable are His judgments and His ways past finding out ! " [2]

[1] Acts xiii. 38, 39.

[2] Rom. xi. 33.

The distinctions here noticed between the different aspects of the work of Christ are clearly marked in the ritual of the Great Day of Atonement (Lev. xvi.)

There were two methods by which the Israelite became identified with his sacrifice, viz., either by laying his hand upon the victim's head before it was killed, as in the case of the ordinary sin-offerings (see pp. 89-90 *ante*); or else by having the blood sprinkled upon him after the victim had been offered, as in the case of various special sacrifices. But in the ritual of the Day of Atonement there was no such identification with the goat " upon which the Lord's lot fell." The ceremonial was entirely to Godward. The blood was carried, not without, to where the people stood, but within, to the presence of God. And the efficacy of that blood to Godward was morally the foundation of the ceremonial respecting the scape-goat, which followed. Aaron, as the appointed representative of the people, laid his hands upon the head of the victim, and " confessed over it all the iniquities of the Children of Israel, and all their transgressions in all their sins, putting them upon the head of the goat," which, as the typical sin-bearer, was then led away " to a land not inhabited." The efficacy *to Godward* of the atonement made through the blood of the first goat was absolute and complete, apart from aught that followed it ; but its practical efficacy to the people depended on their becoming identified with the scape-goat.

And so it is with the antitype. The perfectness of the work of Christ in no way depends upon the benefits which accrue therefrom to the sinner. Whether men receive it or reject it, reconciliation is accomplished, peace is made. But when the sinner believes in

Christ, he enters into peace, he "receives the reconciliation" (Rom. v. 1, 11). Thus becoming identified with Christ, that identification reaches back to His death for sin on Calvary.

Substitution, then, is merely a theological statement of one aspect of this scriptural truth of the believer's oneness with Christ, and if it be taught apart from that truth, it may degenerate into error. The gospel, instead of being a divine revelation, may become a mere problem in metaphysics. Instead of the heart being reached by the stupendous fact that "Christ died for the ungodly," the intellect may seize upon the inference which obviously follows if a forced emphasis be put upon the "*for*." (See Note, p. 95 *ante*.) That the danger is real, witness how many there are in our day who seem to receive the Gospel without any exercise of either heart or conscience.

8

RIGHTEOUSNESS

THE sentence upon sin is death. Man has fallen beneath that sentence ; he is hopelessly, irretrievably doomed. No law-keeping therefore could bring him righteousness : if he is ever to be justified, it must be by the penalty being borne. He must be justified by death, " *justified by blood.*" [1]

Moreover, his spiritual condition is just as hopeless. He *cannot* please God. So then, even if atonement be made for him by another, no blessing can ever reach him unless it come to him in spite of what he is, and not because of any good thing in him. Christ may have died, but the power and value of that death he can never prove, if he must needs raise himself to reach the sphere of its efficacy. He must be justified on some principle as independent of self, as is the blood of the atonement — he must be "*justified by grace.*" [2]

But grace implies that there is no merit in him who is the object of it, no reason whatever in him why he should be blessed. How then, if the blessing be not arbitrarily limited, if it be really " unto all," can a difference be made ? how can one

[1] Rom. v. 9.　　　　　　[2] Rom. iii. 24.

be justified and another not ? It cannot depend on merit ; it cannot depend on effecting a change in one's self ; it cannot depend on doing. It must be simply that one accepts and another rejects a righteousness which is perfect independently of the sinner. How accepts ? how rejects ? accepts by believing, rejects by disbelieving, the testimony of God. " Unto all and upon all them *that believe*." " It is of faith that it may be by grace " : any other ground would be inconsistent with grace. A sinner must be " *justified by faith*." [1]

Death then is the judicial ground of righteousness for a sinner. *Grace* is the principle on which God acts in reckoning him righteous. And it is on the principle of *faith*, as opposed to works or merit, that he receives the blessing.

The death of Christ has, I trust, received due prominence in these pages, and I have already dealt with the great truth of grace, and discussed at length the character of faith. But yet the question of righteousness is of far too great importance to be disposed of thus incidentally. It claims a fuller consideration by the light of Scripture.

And mark, the word is " justified." It is not a question of pardon, merely, but of righteousness. The best of governments might find a reason to pardon the guiltiest inmate of its jails ; but to *justify* a criminal would be morally to become partaker of his crime. And yet, with God, forgiveness is no mere remission of the penalty of sin ; it reaches on, and embraces the justification

---

[1] Rom. v. 1. The Epistle of James speaks of justification by works. Upon this see chap. xii. *post*

of the sinner. Ours is the blessedness of those to whom God imputes righteousness. The believer is pardoned, but that is not all ; he is reckoned righteous. " To him that worketh not, but believeth on Him that justifieth the ungodly, his faith is counted for righteousness." [1]

It is not that God compounds with the sinner, and accepts his faith instead of righteousness ; but that He accounts him righteous, and that in virtue of his faith. The question, How can this be ? is the thesis of the opening chapters of the Epistle to the Romans.

" I am not ashamed of the gospel," the apostle boasts, as he stands by anticipation in the midst of Rome, where power, the power of man, was well-nigh worshipped as divine : " I am not ashamed of the gospel, for it is the power of God unto salvation to every one that believeth, for therein is righteousness which is of God revealed on the principle of faith to faith." [2]

We have thus at the very threshold two import-ant points established : first, that the righteousness with which the believer has to do, is not human but divine ; and, secondly, that it is a new revela-tion. Law and prophets bore witness to it, doubt-less ; but the burden of their testimony was a

[1] Rom. iv. 5.

[2] Rom. i. 17,—" The righteousness of God " is ambiguous, for it may mean the divine attribute, as in chap. iii. 25. And " right-eousness of God," though literally accurate, is too abrupt for our English idiom. I have ventured therefore to render it " righteous-ness which is of God," as idiomatically more correct than the R.V. reading. I suppose it is equivalent to the δ. ἐκ θεοῦ, of Phil. iii. 9.

demand for righteousness from man, whereas the gospel is a revelation of righteousness which is of God. But this revelation was of necessity postponed until the close of the controversy respecting human righteousness. To faith, God did in fact reveal in the old time that there was a divine remedy for man's unrighteousness. It was " witnessed to by the law and the prophets." But to make a public revelation of divine righteousness for man, while the express character of the dispensation was a demand for human righteousness, would be to put a premium upon unrighteousness.[1] The public revelation was a demand for righteousness from man on earth. The alternative was, to faith, forgiveness through divine forbearance ; to unbelief, a warning of judgment to come. But now, in the gospel, human righteousness is set aside for ever, righteousness which is of God is revealed, and the only alternative, and that for all who fail to submit to this righteousness, is wrath of God from heaven.[2]

But is it so clear a case that human righteousness has failed thus signally ? for on this depends

---

[1] Such was precisely the charge brought against the gospel by those who judged it without giving up their standing under " the law and the prophets " (see Rom. iii. 8) ; that is, under the past dispensation, for such is the meaning of the expression. See e.g. Matt. vi. 12, and xxii. 40. To do as we would be done by, is human righteousness, and therefore the Lord says it is " the law and the prophets." So again in the 22nd chapter. This was the special character of the dispensation. See also Luke xvi. 16, which means, not that the Old Testament Scriptures had become obsolete, but that the ministry of John the Baptist inaugurated a change of dispensation.

[2] Rom. i. 18.

the opportuneness of the new revelation. To this, therefore, the apostle forthwith addresses himself.[1]

The creature claimed his liberty, and turned prodigal. God allowed him a long probation to prove what that liberty would lead to, and the result was only evil. Tried by every possible test, man has proved himself to be utterly unrighteous. Left to the light of nature, he turned from it, and proved himself lawless. When the commandment came, he turned against it, and proved himself a transgressor.[2] In the first chapter, the condition of the heathen is depicted in colours dark but true. In the sequel, the exceptional advantages of the Jew are shown to have produced no adequate result.

---

[1] This is the scope of the passage following, *i.e.*, from ver. 19 of chap. i. to ver. 20 of chap. iii. In i. 17 he states the thesis of the doctrinal portion of the Epistle, and returns to it in iii. 21.

[2] To say that man is precisely what God made him to be is sheer blasphemy. "God made man upright." But, it may be urged, God might have made man incapable of sin. That is, He might have created a being destitute of any independent will. Doubtless ; but then such a creature must needs be of a far lower order than Adam and his race. But God might in fact have prevented Adam's sin. That is, He might have created him capable of an independent will, but practically incapable of exercising it. The fact of man's apostasy is a terrible but most signal testimony to the greatness and dignity of the place from which he fell, and it ill becomes him to answer back his Maker, " Why hast Thou made me thus ? " Moreover, God has been vindicated in this respect by the life of Christ on earth ; for such an one as Adam was has perfectly obeyed Him, even in the midst of suffering and sin. Nor is God's goodness at fault towards the fallen race. Man has chosen his own will, and turned from God in the pursuit of it. Let him now return to God, and he will find not only pardon, but blessings far beyond those of which sin has robbed him. But if he refuses grace, either through persisting in his wicked courses, or through going about trying to justify himself, to "establish his own right-eousness " (Rom. x. 3), what can there be for him but wrath ?

And the history of Israel, remember, is the history of human nature tried in the most favourable circumstances. Abraham was of our own flesh and blood. If he differed from other men, it was only that, as judged by men, he was a splendid specimen of the race. God has recorded a mean and wicked act committed by him, for divine biographies are faithful, but the stress that men lay upon this single fault is no common tribute to the character of the patriarch. Abraham's family, therefore, was the little Eden vineyard reclaimed from nature's wildness, and tended and nourished with the utmost care and wisdom.[1] If then, even here, no fitting fruit was yielded, the entire stock may fairly be condemned. If the Jew is shown to have utterly failed, it is the crowning and conclusive proof that Adam's race is evil.

But dreadful as was the outward condition of the heathen, the inward condition of the Jew was just as bad. The first chapter states what man without law openly showed himself to be ; the third chapter records the judgment which God, who reads the heart, has formed of man, even when the restraints of law produced an outward morality. Not that this was any new discovery with God. At the very outset, His judgment of the matter was declared in no doubtful terms.[2] But, in His infinite wisdom, He decreed that the creature should prove it for himself. Now, he has done so. Every

[1] Isa. v. 1–7.
[2] " When men began to multiply on the face of the earth, God saw that the wickedness of man was great in the earth, and that every imagination of the thoughts of his heart was only evil continually " (Gen. vi. 1–5).

mouth, therefore, is stopped, and the whole world has become subject to the judgment of God.[1]   The question of human righteousness is no longer open. Man's period of trial with respect to it is at an end.

Now human righteousness is conformity to law. Not *the* law, for that would limit it to the Jew, and the argument includes both Jew and Gentile ; but to *law* in its wider sense.   God alone is supreme ; the creature must of necessity be subject to law.[2] The law of Sinai was the promulgation, and that for the most part in a negative or penal form, of the standard of creature perfectness, the law of man's nature, as we say.   Murder and theft were as really sinful before the law as after it.   They were forbidden, not to make them wrong, but because they were so.   The Gentile therefore had, by virtue of his very being, the law which at Sinai was formally tabulated in commandments.   Having not *the* law he was a law to himself.[3]   Love to God and man, worked out in the life, is the fulfilment of the law ; it is, moreover, the attainment of creature perfectness.   Indeed, it is the one just because it is the other.   Righteousness then would be the realisation of this.   To express it in the most popular way, it would be man's being exactly what he ought to be.

But the history of Adam's race is God's answer to every pretension of the kind.   As we have

[1] Rom. iii. 19.
[2] Sin is precisely the denial of this   Sin and lawlessness (*ἀνομία* 1 John iii. 4) are convertible times.   See p. 143 *post.*
[3] Rom. ii. 14.

already seen, man's probation is at an end. The door is shut upon human righteousness altogether. It is not that by the deeds of the law, they who had the law can no longer be justified; but that by deeds of law,[1] upon that principle in any sense, no *flesh living* can be justified.

At the cost of repeating myself, I must insist on this, that man is in this sense no longer in a state of probation at all. That era God has finally brought to an end. The Holy Spirit has come, not to reopen the question of sin and righteousness and judgment, but to convince the world that it is closed for ever.[2] If then human righteousness—righteousness on the principle of conformity to law, the principle, namely, of man's being what he ought to be—is irrevocably set aside, there must be a revelation of righteousness which is of God, and therefore, of course, on some principle altogether different. " But now, *apart from law*," the apostle proceeds, " righteousness which is of God is revealed,

[1] Rom. iii. 20, ἐξ ἔργων νόμου. On this, see Bloomfield and the authorities cited by him, whom I have followed. Alford's reason for departing from them (*i.e.* " that no such general idea of *law* seems to have ever been before the mind of the apostle ") is not only a flagrant instance of *petitio principii*, but certainly wrong. See *e.g.* Rom. vii. 8. " Without law sin is dead," is a great and important principle. But the statement that " without the law sin was dead," is not only incorrect, but opposed to the apostle's teaching in chap. ii. 14, 15. " With the article, νόμος invariably denotes the Mosaic law, except when its meaning is limited by accompanying words. Without the article, in cases where the omission is not required by grammatical rule, the term appears to have a wider significance; sometimes referring to the Mosaic law as the type of law in general, and sometimes to law in the abstract, including every form of divine command or moral obligation." (S. G. Green's *Handbook to the Grammar of the Greek Testament*, § 234.)

[2] John xvi. 8–11.

being borne witness to by the law and the prophets."[1] Hitherto, human righteousness has been demanded ; but now, divine righteousness is revealed. We shall see presently what the principle is on which it is based ; but here, we have the point settled, that it is not on the principle of law. " By deeds of law no flesh living can be justified " ; righteousness is now on a wholly different ground. The contrast is not between personal and vicarious law-keeping, but between righteousness on the principle of law-keeping, and righteousness which is entirely apart from law ; between righteousness of man, worked out on earth, and righteousness of God, revealed from heaven.

But righteousness is a complex word. It expresses either a personal moral quality or a judicial state. If any one be personally righteous, he is, of course, and by virtue of it, judicially righteous also. On the other hand, to declare a person to be judicially righteous who personally is *not* righteous, is, according to human judgment, unrighteous and immoral. But God has done this very thing, and the great wonder of the gospel is how He could do it. How can God be just, and yet the Justifier of ungodly sinners ? Here is the great problem of our Epistle.

To say that, although man has broken the law, God regards him as having kept it, is no solution of it. It is not an *answer* to the difficulty ; it shelves it altogether. If a man keep the law, or,

---

[1] Rom. iii. 21 ; νυνὶ δὲ χωρὶς νόμου δ. " But *now* (*i.e.* under the present dispensation), a method of justification appointed by God, without reference to (lit., apart from) obedience to law of any kind, is revealed."—BLOOMFIELD.

what comes to the same thing, if God deem him to have kept it, he is justified on that ground, and there is no room and no need for justification through redemption. If righteous living, whether personal or vicarious, can bring righteousness, then righteousness comes by law, and Christ need not have died.[1] But righteousness on that ground is shown to be impossible, and righteousness which is of God is revealed—righteousness on a wholly different principle. If God looks upon the believer as having kept the law there is an end of the whole matter, for to *declare* a person righteous who *is* righteous is simply a matter of course. But the great marvel of the gospel, the great triumph of redemption, is that God can declare those to be righteous who personally are not righteous ; that He can justify the sinner, not by deeming him a law-keeper, but even while He judges him as a law-breaker. It is not that, being justified by the life of Christ on earth, we are saved by His blood-shedding ; but that, " being now justified by His blood, we shall be saved from wrath through Him," as now risen from the dead.[2] We are justified without a cause, by God's grace, through the redemption that is in Christ Jesus.[3]

But, as we have already seen, the gospel of this righteousness was a new revelation. In the old time, God demanded righteousness from man, and pronounced a death-sentence upon sin. And yet saint after saint, from Abel downwards, went to heaven, though unrighteous, and in spite of sin.

---

[1] Εἰ γὰρ διὰ νόμου δ. ἄρα Χριστὸς δωρεὰν ἀπέθανεν. Gal. ii. 21.
[2] Rom. v. 9.   [3] Rom. iii. 24.

Instead of death they found forgiveness. How then about the righteousness of God ? The law and the prophets bore witness that it would be manifested, but it remained a hidden mystery. The whole question of God's righteousness was in abeyance. But now, the time has come for bringing all things into light. God has not only manifested righteousness for the sinner : He has set forth Christ, to declare and vindicate His own. " Whom God set forth," the chapter proceeds, " to be a propitiation, through faith, by His blood, to show His righteousness, because of the passing over of the sins done aforetime, in the forbearance of God." [1]

It is no mere question here of a judicial standing-ground for the sinner, great though that question be, but the personal character of God Himself. So clear is the case against even the best of Adam's sons in the judgment of all the great intelligences of the universe, so evil and polluted is this wretched race of ours, that God thinks fit to vindicate His character in stooping to take up our cause. All darkness now is past ; the day of full revelation has dawned. God loved His people in the old time, for God is love ; but that love was *manifested* when " God sent His only-begotten Son into the world." He spared not His Son, but freely gave Him up.

Nor would a higher wisdom have found an easier redemption, nor sterner righteousness have

[1] Rom. iii. 25, R.V. Alford remarks, " Observe, πάρεσις is not forgiveness, but *overlooking*, which is the work of *forbearance* (see Acts xvii. 30) ; whereas *forgiveness* is the work of *grace* (see chapter ii. 4) ; nor is τῶν προγεγ. ἁμ., ' the sins of each man which precede his conversion,' but *those of the whole world before the death of Christ.* See the very similar words, Heb. ix. 15."

required a fuller satisfaction. *Now* is made known unto principalities and powers in heavenly places, the manifold wisdom of God.[1] *Now*, before earth and heaven, is declared His righteousness. " To declare, I say," the apostle repeats, to give it fitting emphasis : " to declare, at this time, His righteousness, that He might be just, and the justifier of him that believeth in Jesus."

Heaven peopled with the lost of earth, might well seem proof of God's weakness in forgiving, were it not that it is " the Lamb as it had been slain," who now fills the throne. The blood-stained mercy-seat above is the sinner's hope, his only right to enter there. The blood - stained mercy - seat is God's eternal witness to His own great attribute of righteousness. That blood is at once the sinner's justification, and the proof that God Himself is just.[2] When God imputed sin to Christ, He became so thoroughly identified with it that the Word declares " He was made sin for us." When God now imputes His righteousness to the believer, we become so thoroughly identified therewith that the Word declares we are "made the righteousness of God in Christ."[3]

But wonderful though this be, it will be asked, is even this enough ? Must not the sinner have the personal quality of righteousness, as well as the judicial, to fit him for the presence of God ?[4]

[1] Eph. iii. 10.
[2] As regards the typical meaning of " blood " see chap. xv. *post.*
[3] 2 Cor. v. 21.
[4] These are distinguished by divines as negative and positive righteousness. The latter is closely allied to sanctification, but it must by no means be confounded with it, as is commonly done.

Undoubtedly he must ; and the question arises, What is the ground and source of it ? But here, remember, we reach beyond the scope of the Scriptures we have been considering. The first four chapters of Romans deal with the great question of forensic righteousness ; now we pass from the forensic altogether. It is a question of moral fitness. The redeemed sinner must be not merely justified, he must be righteous morally and in fact. In the picture of a parable, or the poetry of prophecy, judicial righteousness may fitly be represented as a " wedding garment," or a " robe " ; [1] but here the question is, What lies beneath that robe, that garment ? not the wearer's title to be where he is, but his fitness for the place he holds by virtue of that title.[2]

Sin unexpiated must be an insuperable barrier between the sinner and his God. Love and grace there may be, and pity for his ruin ; but righteousness forbids their exercise, so long as ever its requirements are unsatisfied. But, by the death of Christ, the believer is released from every claim and penalty pertaining to his former state. He is redeemed, bought back by God, and is, now,

[1] The doctrinal importance attached so generally to the expression " robe of righteousness " in the 61st of Isaiah, is one of the many strange phenomena of theology. The expression used in the 59th chapter might naturally have been expected to claim far more notice, on account of its being adopted in the New Testament. (Eph. vi. 14.)

[2] The point of the parable of the Marriage Supper (Matt. xxii.) is not that the man was unbidden, nor that he was personally unfit for the scene ; but that, relying on his personal qualifications, he dispensed with the wedding garment. He had such an opinion of himself, that he thought he might attend court in his ordinary dress. It is the sinner, because of his personal righteousness, refusing " to submit to the righteousness of God."

absolutely God's. Pity, now, may stoop to save, and love and grace may flow unhindered. God may lavish blessings on the ransomed sinner. And He may raise him to what place He will.[1] He may either repair the ruin of the Adam race, and restore the old creation, marred by sin ; or else, dethroning him who is the head of that creation and that race, He may introduce the sinner into a new sphere altogether. And Scripture is not silent here, nor does it speak in doubtful terms.

The pattern to which all the sons of faith are yet to be conformed, is not Adam in Eden innocence, but the risen Christ at the right hand of God. For neither circumcision, nor yet uncircumcision now avails, " but a new creation " ;[2] and the believer's fitness for the home that is before him, depends upon the perfectness of Christ as Head of that creation, and his own part therein by virtue of his oneness with Him. It is not in His work we are accepted, but in Himself, and yet not in Himself as separated from His work. The Christ who now sits upon the throne is the Christ of Calvary, and the Christ of Calvary is the Jesus of Bethlehem

---

[1] Justification is in no sense a believer's title to heaven, nor yet his fitness to be there. If British law justify an accused person, he walks forth free ; but he does not gain thereby a right to live in Windsor Castle, nor any fitness for such a position. He may already possess the title and the moral qualities befitting it ; but these are wholly independent of his acquittal, though upon it might depend his power to profit by them. The same grace which justifies a sinner is itself the source of every blessing the justified enjoys.

[2] Gal. vi. 15. That is, it is no longer a question of human perfectness, whether according to the standard of the law of nature, or of the revelation of it made at Sinai ; but of passing out from that entire position, and gaining a new standing-ground in Christ.

and Bethany. There can be no union with Him save in resurrection, and we can have no part whatever in His life on earth until first we have been made one with Him in that death which justifies. But, once united to Him, we stand accepted in all the perfectness of everything He is, and of everything He has ever proved Himself to be. " If any man be in Christ, he is a new creature : old things are passed away ; behold, all things are become new." The Only-begotten Son has not come down to patch up the ruined fabric of the old creation ; but, closing its history for ever by His death, to bring the redeemed of earth into a new creation of which He, the Lord from heaven, is the Head. " He is made unto us from God wisdom, and both righteousness and sanctification, even (complete) redemption." [1]

By the light of the full and final revelation of the gospel, I have thus sought to find the answer to the problem left unsolved upon one of the earliest pages of Holy Writ : " How should man be just with God ? " [2] I have shown how the sinner can alone be justified—justified not on the principle of law obeyed, but on the principle of sin condemned ; " justified freely by His grace through the redemption that is in Christ Jesus." [3] Having thus described the sure foundation of the believer's blessedness in Christ, I, have gone on to speak of full salvation yet to be realised in glory, when " the new man which after God is created in righteousness and holiness of truth," [4] will be displayed in all the

---

[1] 1 Cor. i. 30.   See note p. 172 *post*.

[2] Job ix. 2.

[3] Rom. iii. 24.   See chap. xiii. *post*.

[4] Eph. iv. 24.

perfectness of Him who is the Head of that new creation.

And now I close the chapter, for my task is done. But I could wish that some worthier pen were here to fill the page with exhortations fitting such a theme. If such be the Christian's past, and such his destiny, what a present should be his ! Blameless before his fellow-men, as by grace he has been freed from every charge before his God. Marked by strict, unswerving uprightness in all his ways on earth, for he is destined one day to be conformed to the image of Christ in glory. "For the grace of God hath appeared, bringing salvation to all men, instructing us to the intent that, denying ungodliness and worldly lusts, we should live soberly, and righteously, and godly in this present world ; looking for the blessed hope, and appearing of the glory of our great God and Saviour Jesus Christ ; who gave Himself for us, that He might redeem us from all iniquity, and purify unto Himself a people for His own possession, zealous of good works." [1]

[1] Tit. ii. 11-13. The Revised Version, from which the above is quoted, seems even more definitely than the Authorised Version to make σωτήριος predicate after ἐπεφάνη. The teaching of the passage, however, is not that God's grace in fact brings salvation to all men, but that such is its character and intention. This is clear in the original, but it is not easily conveyed in English. The text might be rendered thus : " The grace of God, salvation-bringing to all men, hath appeared, disciplining us," etc. (See p. 80 *ante*.)

9

SANCTIFICATION

WE have thus seen how a sinner is once and for ever justified, when he believes in Christ, and stands thenceforth righteous before God, beyond every demand of law and every charge of sin. We have seen further how the personal moral quality which is akin to such a standing, pertains to the new creation in which the believer has his place. And, in conclusion, we have noticed how practical conformity to that standing, and cultivation of that quality, are characteristic of true Christian life. All this, moreover, springs from, and rests upon the truth that God is righteous.

But God is not only righteous, He is also holy ; and every requirement of righteousness has its correlative claim in regard to holiness. Sin not only brings the sinner before the judgment seat, it excludes him from the sanctuary. He is not only guilty, but defiled. And though faith accepts the blessings that are ours in Christ, and humbly takes the place they give, and the heart presses forward to the day of full redemption, when the redeemed shall be presented faultless before God ; yet, sure and full though the blessing be, and bright and clear the hope, the sad stern facts around us and within are no less real. Sinners in a world of sin, though justified, and born of God, and on our way to certain glory, how can we pray and serve and worship, here on earth, for God is holy ? It is not a question, now, of our place in Christ at God's right hand, nor yet of a new nature by virtue of a new birth from heaven. It is what we know ourselves to be as we walk the streets or fall upon our knees to pray ; ourselves, the responsible living persons in whom this new nature dwells. How can *we* approach a holy, holy, holy God ?

In the Epistle to the Romans, the scene was laid in the hall of judgment. The righteous God was on the throne. At the bar there stood the sinner, guilty, condemned, and silent. The righteous sentence had gone forth, and he had not a word to offer why it should not be fulfilled. And we saw how, when all hope was dead, sovereign grace could justify the guilty even as he stood, and call him from the very bar of judgment to fellowship with Christ in glory.

But now we turn to the Epistle to the Hebrews, and here a new scene presents itself. The centre object is a holy shrine, and not the throne of righteousness. It is surrounded, not by lost and guilty outcasts, but by a redeemed and happy people. They are in the wilderness, however, beset by need and infirmity and sin. But they have a great leader to provide for need on the journey to the rest before them, and a priest to help their infirmities and to make atonement for their sin. The priest is theirs in virtue of a covenant, and the covenant has also a sanctuary, an altar, and a sacrifice. Here then we have a people exactly like ourselves, in circumstances like our own. For our present difficulty is not at all how redemption can be obtained, or a home in heaven made sure; that question has been set at rest. But it is as to the place redemption gives us during our sojourn here on earth, and the provision made to maintain us in this place, seeing we are weak, and wayward, and sinful, and in circumstances of difficulty and trial. Let us seek then, by the help of the typical history of Israel, to trace out the truth we are in search of for ourselves.

But, first of all, let this be clearly settled, that Israel's redemption was accomplished ere ever they sang their hymn of triumph upon the wilderness shore of the sea. Their redemption depended solely on the passover in Egypt, and the waves that rolled between them and the House of Bondage—death in its spiritual significance, and death in its separating power. It was in no respect, therefore, the work of priesthood, or the result of priestly sacrifice. The sacrifice of the passover was not a priestly act. Priesthood pertained to the covenant, and this was not an ordinance of the covenant at all. The yearly festival which the covenant enjoined was but a memorial celebration of the one great passover of their redemption; and it was as thus redeemed that Jehovah entered into covenant with them. We must remember therefore, that in following Israel's story, the moment we turn the page of the 12th chapter of the Book of Exodus, we are dealing with a people whose pressing need was not redemption but SANCTIFICATION

Here, then, is precisely the point at which we have ourselves arrived in this inquiry. Let us pursue the matter further, and seek to ascertain how Israel was sanctified, and thus to discern the truth with reference to ourselves. Israel was a redeemed people. But God had a purpose in their redemption, and that purpose had yet to be fulfilled. He redeemed them from Egypt and from the power of Pharaoh, that He might establish them as a holy people in covenant with Himself. Covenant was based upon redemption, and followed as an inseparable consequence.[1] But the covenant was inaugurated with the blood of burnt-offerings and peace-offerings sacrificed to Jehovah, and it was by the blood of the covenant, sprinkled on the people, that their sanctification was accomplished. Thus it was that they were introduced into the place to which they were entitled by virtue of redemption, and became in fact what they were already by the promise and purpose of their God.[2]

Christ is the great Paschal Lamb of our redemption. He is also the Burnt-offering of the covenant. We are "redeemed with the precious blood of Christ, as of a lamb without blemish and without spot." "We are sanctified by the offering of the body of Jesus Christ once for all."[3] The covenant

---

[1] Truth has many sides, but here I am dealing with but one. In one sense redemption is a result of covenant, and here sanctification precedes it ; for the meaning of sanctification is a setting apart for God. But in another sense, redemption is the foundation of covenant, and sanctification follows as a consequence. Both these seem to be included in the opening words of 1 Pet. : " Elect through sanctification of the Spirit unto sprinkling of the blood of Jesus Christ."

[2] Ex. xxiv.   [3] 1 Pet. i. 19 ; Heb. x. 10.

is inseparable from redemption, and it is by the blood of the covenant that the believer is sanctified. And this is no mere form of words, no piece of idle rhetoric. Sanctification was a reality for Israel. Without it, there could have been no covenant, no priest, no sanctuary. And it is likewise a reality with us, and just as necessary. It is as much a fact as our justification, and as absolute and complete. By nature not righteous but guilty, we have seen how the sinner is justified. By nature not holy but defiled, he is likewise sanctified.

And both depend alike, and only, upon blood. He is righteous, moreover, because God has declared him righteous ; and it is by the call of God that he is holy. " And such were some of you," the apostle reminds the Corinthian Christians, after naming transgressors of the grossest kind, " but ye are washed, but ye are sanctified, but ye are justified " : [1] " Sanctified in Christ Jesus, called saints," as he had described them in the salutation of the epistle.[2]

Sanctification in this sense, therefore, is not a gradual change or a progressive work, nor yet a moral attribute ; it is an act, like justification, accomplished once for all.[3] Just as the guilty sinner passes, immediately when he believes, into a new condition relatively to sin and a righteous God, and becomes thereby and thenceforth

[1] I Cor. vi. 11.
[2] I Cor. i. 2. Not " called to be saints," but constituted saints by the call of God.
[3] See chap. xiv. *post.*

righteous ; so the defiled sinner gains, as immedi‑
ately and in the same way, a new standing rel‑
atively to sin and a holy God, and becomes thereby
and thenceforth holy. "Whatsoever God doeth,
it shall be for ever : nothing can be put to it, nor
anything taken from it." [1]

But it will doubtless be argued, However true
and blessed this may be, it fails to satisfy our
need, for this is only the setting out upon our
pilgrimage ; and though perfectly sanctified when
we believe, we may soon become defiled again.
What provision then has been made to keep us
holy on the way ? This is precisely what we learn,
in part by comparison and in part by contrast,
from the Epistle to the Hebrews. And here let me
give the reader a threefold clew to the seeming
difficulties which make that wonderful and blessed
book so profitless to many. Judaism, first of all,
is here regarded not as the apostate faith which
crucified Messiah, but as that holy religion whose
aim and work it was to lead to Him. The true
Israelite had no need to be *converted* to Christianity.
He had already, as a Jew, experienced the new
birth of water and the Spirit, without which no one
can see the kingdom ; [2] and he accepted Christ,
not as the founder of a new religion, but as the
author and fulfiller of the true and holy faith which
had already knit his soul to God. It is to such
that the book is especially addressed. Secondly, the
believer is looked at, not as seated in the heavens
in Christ,[3] but as here on earth ; nor yet as a member
of His Body, but as one of a company of " holy

[1] Eccles. iii. 14.   [2] See note p. 66 *ante.*   [3] Eph. ii. 6.

brethren, partakers of a heavenly calling," setting out on their wilderness journey home. And thirdly, the book takes up our spiritual history at the point which Israel had reached in the 24th chapter of Exodus. Redemption is complete. The covenant has been established. The people have been sanctified. And having thus made purification for sins, the Mediator of the covenant is gone up to God.[1]

And here it is that priesthood meets us. As yet we have known no priestly functions. It was not a priestly hand that killed the passover, or sprinkled the door of the dwelling with its blood. It was not a priestly hand that sacrificed the dedication offering of the covenant ; and the sanctification of the people was the work of the mediator, not of the priest. It is as " brought again from the dead, in virtue of the blood of the everlasting covenant," and now passed into the heavens, purification for sin being made, that the Son of God has been proclaimed a Priest.[2]

[1] Compare Ex. xxiv. 8, 9, with Heb. i. 3.

[2] Here the type fails us. Moses went up to the Mount as mediator of the covenant, and would then have been called to the priesthood, had not the offices become separated, owing to his want of faith (Ex. iv. 14). Aaron, therefore, was made priest ; but it was then, and not before, that he received the call. His formal consecration was still later. See Lev. viii. ix., which is connected with Ex. xxiv., and gives us the fulfilment of that which took place on the Mount. And mark that it was Moses who officiated in regard of these offerings (comp. Ex. xxix.) ; and further, that he was associated with Aaron in the act which typified Christ's coming forth hereafter as Royal Priest to bless His people (Lev. ix. 23).

It is most important to see that the Lord's priesthood dates from His enthronement in heaven. See Heb. ii. 17 (where the

We have thus not only a great leader,—the Captain of our salvation, and a home to which He guides ; but if through sin or frailty we fail to follow Him aright, and turn aside or stumble by the way, we know Him also as a great High Priest, who can sympathise and help. He can sympathise, for He was in all points tried as we are ; He can help, for the trial found no sin.[1]

But to offer sacrifices for sins was Aaron's peculiar vocation. There are other priestly functions different from this, and higher ; but this was the characteristic of the Aaronic order. It was founded on the necessity for. expiation. If then the sacrifice had in fact accomplished the work it typified, and sin had been put away, there would have been no need for the priesthood of the law. A priest there must have been truly, for there can be no worship without a priest and a sanctuary ; but not a priest of the Aaronic type. Faith grasped the truth which the sacrifice prefigured ; but sin was not, in fact, put away, and therefore, on account of the inefficacy of the blood with which they had to do, there was a remembrance again of sins continually, and every transgression demanded

word is " that He might *become* ") ; v. 5–10, vi. 20, vii. 23, 24, viii. 1–4. He *could not* be a priest while on earth (Heb. viii. 4). See chap. xvi. *post.*

[1] Heb. iv. 15. Our English Version is ambiguous here, and the words have been very generally perverted to mean that the Lord's temptations were exactly similar to ours, the *result* alone being different. Were this so, He must have known the power of sin within—the source of so many of our trials. But the words are χωρὶς ἁμαρτίας, *apart from sin.* " So that throughout these temptations, in their origin, in their process, in their result,—sin had nothing in Him : He was free and separate from it " (Alford).

a new sacrifice to maintain them in holiness befitting the covenant.

But now, by the death of Christ, expiation has been accomplished, sin has been purged, and not only is the worshipper sanctified, but the sanctified ones are perfected for ever. There is therefore no longer room for sacrifice, no need henceforth for blood-shedding. The Aaronic priesthood is at an end ; the priesthood of the Son of God is of a different order altogether,—the order of Melchisedec. But the priesthood is connected with the covenant ; and if the one be changed, the other follows as of course.[1] And it is with the new covenant that the believer has to do, a covenant in keeping with the priesthood of Melchisedec, a covenant based on the great fact that sins and iniquities are for ever expiated, and on the promise that God will remember them no more. To the covenant, again, there pertains a sanctuary. The sanctuary of the old covenant bore witness by its very structure that there was a place of access still closed against the worshipper, and " a greater and more perfect tabernacle " yet to be revealed. The new covenant and the priesthood of Christ have to do with this the true tabernacle in heaven itself.

Ours, therefore, is an eternal redemption, and an everlasting covenant ; we have the Son of God Himself as the Apostle and High Priest of our profession, the Holiest in the heavens as our sanctuary, and the blood of Christ to perfect us, and make us fit for such a shrine. If, then, the

[1] Heb. vii. 12.

question should still be pressed, What have we further that is akin to the great yearly sin-offering of the law, and the offerings for trespasses and sins of ignorance ? I answer, the need of these repeated sacrifices arose entirely from the inefficacy of the blood of the covenant to which they pertained ; but the blood of the new covenant has brought us remission fully and absolutely, and, " where remission of these is, there is no more offering for sin." We have seen how, when once justified by blood, we stand in perfect righteousness ; so now we see how, once sanctified by blood, we stand in holiness as absolute and perfect.

But though sin can no longer master the sacrifice which purges it, and is as powerless to exclude us from the sanctuary as to drag us into judgment, still we are in daily contact with what defiles ; is there then no need for cleansing ? There is truly, and full provision for it, too, through the same death which justifies. Every ordinance of the old covenant that was required by reason of the " weakness and unprofitableness " of the sacrifices, we are for ever done with ; but there was a special rite to meet the need that was inseparable from the circumstances of the people, and this has its abiding antitype for us. A Jew of blameless life might possibly have had no cause to resort to the offerings for sins and trespasses ; yet he could not on that ground absent himself upon the great day of atonement, for that depended on the inherent inefficiency of the sacrifice. But even if sin had been fully purged, and the worshipper absolutely sinless, he would have been none the less liable at any moment to become defiled ; for under the ceremonial law the Israelite became unclean by contact with death in any form. And this defilement was met by water, not by blood. But it was by water which owed its efficacy to a sacrifice accomplished. I allude, of course, to the offering of the red heifer, enjoined in the 19th chapter of Numbers. The victim was led forth without the camp, where it was slain and burnt to ashes, part of the blood being first brought in and sprinkled before the tabernacle of the congregation. The ashes were then laid up outside the camp, and water that had touched those ashes availed to purify. The Israelite who had become unclean was sprinkled with this " water of separation," and then, having washed his clothes, and bathed his person, he was cleansed from the defilement.

It is impossible that the blood of Christ can do less than make perfect the sinner whom it sanctifies ; but, even in the case of those who are so richly blest, there can be no fellowship with a holy God, no access to His presence, if that be allowed which is opposed to Him. The touch of evil cannot but defile ; and if we insist that there is no need to come back again to blood, it is not that we make light of sin, but that we pay due homage to the sacrifice that has once and for ever purged it. The blood has achieved its work ; our future cleansing results from " the water of the Word," as applied by the Holy Ghost.[1] The sprinkling of the water which had flowed over the ashes of the sacrifice, typified our bringing the

[1] See chap. xv. *post.*

Spirit's testimony about the death of Christ to bear upon ourselves in regard to that which has defiled us. The washing which followed upon that sprinkling is the clearing ourselves practically from the evil. It is not enough to judge the evil while continuing in it ; it is not enough to turn from it, however zealously, without having to do with God respecting it. But to turn from it, even as we judge it in the presence of the Cross by that Word which is sharper than a two-edged sword, is to bring us face to face with a Priest whose work secures to us divine compassion, and the grace our weakness needs.[1]

And here it is, indeed, that true priestly work begins. I have already noticed that Israel was not only redeemed, but brought into covenant with God, and sanctified, apart from priesthood ; and in the 19th chapter of Numbers, we have again a sacrifice and a rite in which the high-priest took no part. And this is the more remarkable because these, the three great sacrifices that were not sacerdotal, were precisely those which were offered once for all, and could never be repeated.[2]

The death of Christ was not a priestly sacrifice. It was the *foundation* of the covenant, and, as I have already said, it is to the covenant that priesthood

---

[1] Heb. iv. 12–16. 1 John teaches a kindred truth. Confession and advocacy are the correlatives of washing and priesthood. The one has to do with the Father's house, the other with " the house of God," *i.e.*, the sanctuary. Christ is " a Son over His own house " ; He is " a Priest over the house of God." We *are* the household of the Son ; we have access to the house of God (Heb. iii. 6, and x. 21).

[2] See chap. xvi. *post*, and especially the last paragraph.

pertains. It was " after He had made purification for sins and sat down at the right hand of the Majesty on high " that the Son of God was proclaimed a Priest. Purification by blood, as we have seen, was not priestly work, but the prerogative of the Mediator of the covenant. The purification by water was the work of neither priest nor mediator ; and in keeping with the truth that any hand could sprinkle the water of separation, there is the exhortation, " Let us cleanse *ourselves* from all filthiness of the flesh and spirit." [1]

---

[1] 2 Cor. vii. 1. I have said that Hebrews teaches us partly by contrast and partly by comparison ; and in exemplification of that remark I may here give another key to that Epistle, and a clew by which to follow aright the teaching of the types. Everything pertaining to the old covenant, which existed in virtue of some unchanging principle, or of the condition and circumstances of the people, finds its exact correlative in the new covenant. But on the other hand, with respect to all in the old covenant that depended on the powerlessness of the ordinance, the inefficacy of the sacrifice, we learn from the absence of any antitype the perfectness of the new. They had a sanctuary, and so have we. But the veil that divided theirs is rent for us, and the holiest is open. Christ is the fulfilment of the great sacrifices I have enumerated ; but if we turn to seek the antitype of their continually repeated sin-offerings, we are reminded by their absence of the virtue of the blood shed on Calvary. They had a priest, as we have. But Aaron's special work arose from the special need which now has been for ever satisfied. The priesthood of the Son therefore is of another order. To make intercession and reconciliation for sins, and to offer gifts and sacrifices, here are the functions which belong essentially to priesthood : it was the peculiarity of the Aaronic priesthood that the sacrifices they offered were for *sins*. Our great High Priest has no need to sacrifice for sins. He did this once for all ere ever His priesthood was proclaimed. But, like Melchisedec of old, He receives and offers up to God the gifts of the believer's service and the sacrifice of his praise and worship, feeding him in return with the bread and wine of heaven, and crowning all with the blessing of His God (Gen. xiv. 18-20)

But the words which follow those I have this moment cited remind me that what I have said of righteousness is no less true of holiness : the word has various meanings.   When we predicate of some one that he is *holy*, we may be giving expression, if we are speaking in scriptural language, to any one of three ideas, which, though allied, are by no means inseparable.   We may mean that he is one of those who have been sanctified by the blood of Christ, or in other words that he is a Christian.   All such are holy in a sense both true and deep, irrespective of their conduct.[1]

But a holy person may become defiled, even as were the Corinthian saints at the very time the apostle wrote to them.   They had been made holy in Christ Jesus, and were holy by their calling, but yet they were unclean through dreadful sin unjudged among them.   I may speak of holiness therefore as describing a life, or practical condition, in keeping with the Christian's calling.   He is holy and separated to God by virtue of his calling : his daily life ought to be in accordance therewith. Christians are holy persons ; they ought therefore to live " as becometh holy persons " ;[2] they ought to be holy in this practical and secondary sense.

---

[1] " Holy ones " or " saints," for the words are identical in the Greek, οἱ ἅγιοι, is in Scripture the ordinary title of the saved.   The name of " Christian " was probably coined by the people of Antioch who were noted for that propensity.   (See Alford and Bloomfield on Acts xi. 26.)   It is used only in Acts xxvi. 28 (*by Agrippa*), and in 1 Pet. iv. 16.   As Christianity was not a lawful religion, a Christian was as chargeable under Roman law, as was a thief or an agitator (*allotrioepiskopos.*)

[2] Eph. v. 3.

But it will be observed that in both these senses, holiness describes a relation rather than a quality ; it represents a condition, not an attribute. And this brings us to a third meaning of the word, a meaning which it bears in the verse already quoted · " Let us cleanse ourselves from all filthiness of the flesh and spirit, perfecting holiness in the fear of the Lord." " *Perfecting* holiness," observe ; proving that the holiness he speaks of is incomplete and capable of degrees. Therefore he is not speaking here of attaining holiness by the blood, nor yet of maintaining ourselves in the position into which it brings us, but of cultivating in a practical way the character akin to such a state.[1]

Now, in either of the senses in which hitherto I have used the word, to speak of incomplete holiness or sanctification, is a mere contradiction in terms. An unconverted person is absolutely unholy, and a Christian is absolutely holy. That, in virtue of the blood, the Christian is perfectly and for ever holy, is the most prominent truth of the Epistle to the Hebrews. " Christ has perfected for ever them that are sanctified." And again, in its secondary sense, holiness admits of no degrees. Here it is not advancing that we speak of, but *continuing* in holiness.[2] The Israelite who touched defilement became not *less* holy, but unholy ; and, until his purification was accomplished, he was absolutely unclean ; but, when the rite was fulfilled, he became immediately and absolutely clean.

---

[1] It is a different form of word that is here used. (See chap. **xiv**. *post.*)

[2] 1 Tim. ii. 15

If we forget this, we shall be betrayed into light and sinful thoughts of God. Lovingly to touch a dead wife's hand, excluded the Jew as absolutely from the tabernacle, as would her blood if in guilty anger he had shed it.[1] It was a severe and stern enactment, and must seem more than strange to those who fail to see its spiritual significance. There is no question of degrees in the holiness of a thrice holy God. It is not that great sins shut the sinner out, while allowance can be made for trifling faults. Perfection is the only standard that can avail with Him; and full provision has been made, not only to make us, but to keep us, perfect.

But yet, in saying this, we stand at an immeasurable distance from all the low thoughts of God, and light views of sin, that alone can lend an air of plausibility to such a delusion as that any cultivation of piety, or attainment in sanctity, can ever give us right to seek His presence, or fitness to be there. It is only and altogether in virtue of the blood of Christ that the saintliest saint on earth can hold fellowship with God. A higher title is impossible, and no lower will avail.

But this holiness is merely the correlative of

[1] An Israelite became defiled either by sin, or by touching what was unclean. Blood was needed to purge him in the one case, but the water availed in the other. But the necessity for blood arose from the inefficacy of the sacrifice. If the worshipper had been really purged, he would never have needed to come back to blood at all (see Heb. x. 2); and in that case the "water of separation" might perhaps have taken the place of the sin and trespass offerings in cases within the 4th, 5th, and 6th chaps. of Leviticus. It is not that sin has become less heinous than it was under the law (see chap. x. *post*), but that the blood of Christ has in fact accomplished purification.

forensic[1] righteousness. "Merely," I say, not to make little of it, for the one is as real and as essential as the other, but because something more is needed for the home of God. No one shall be there who is not *intrinsically* holy.[2] And here I would beg the reader to turn back to the preceding chapter, and to read the latter part again, substituting holiness for righteousness throughout. Our moral fitness for heaven, in this respect as in the other, is independent of attainments achieved on earth. As regards rewards for faithfulness and service upon earth, no two of the redeemed, it may be, will stand upon a level ; but the perfectness of the new creation will be shared alike by all. The standard is not what the Christian becomes by the work of the Spirit, here, but what Christ now is as seated at the right hand of God. I cite the words again, The new man " is created in righteousness and *holiness* of truth." [3] No change of scene can add virtue to the blood of Christ, therefore heaven itself can add nothing to the holiness in which we stand by reason of that blood. No holy living upon earth can add to the intrinsic perfectness of Christ Himself ; therefore it can add nothing to the holiness which shall be ours when made like unto Him who is the head of the new creation.

[1] I know of no corresponding word in this connection. *Ceremonial* holiness would give the direction of the thought, but entirely fail of conveying its force.

[2] I use the popular expression without stopping to consider its *accuracy*, for it means a right thing.

[3] Eph. iv. 24. The words imply that these are qualities inherent in the new man in virtue of his very creation. It is not ἁγιασμός, therefore, which is here used, but ὁσιότης. (See chap. xiv. *post.*)

I have thus endeavoured to unfold, and establish on the authority of Scripture, the truth of the believer's absolute and perfect sanctification in Christ. I have also spoken of what I may venture to term *continuous* sanctification, the constant conformity to that standard in his life on earth. Thirdly, I have alluded, though still more briefly, as being still further beyond the scope of my subject, to *progressive* sanctification, the cultivation of holiness as a moral quality. And lastly, I have shown that the sinner's meetness for heaven in this respect, as in regard of righteousness, depends not on attainment here, but on his perfectness as a part of the new creation in Christ.

And now it is once more with a feeling of reluctance that I lay down my pen. I cannot but fear lest the great truth I have sought to unfold should suffer in the estimation of some, through being divorced from practical exhortations to a holy life. But I take comfort from the hope that thoughtful minds will in no way share the prejudice. Valuable though exhortation be, truth has a power independent of the appeals we base upon it ; and, therefore, no teaching that is truly doctrinal can fail to be likewise practical. In dealing with this subject I have already gone somewhat beyond the due limits of my theme, which is the gospel, and not the Christian life ; but I have struggled in vain to keep within them.

The unusual interest which the doctrine of holiness excites, combined with the fact that the great truth of sanctification by blood is unknown to our creeds, and but little noticed in our religious literature, has not only made the task important, but has vastly increased my difficulties in the effort to fulfil it. I now dismiss it with a parting word. Even by those who own it, this truth is sometimes spoken of as though it were a fiction or a theory. But with the Israelite his sanctification was one of the most true and solemn facts of his existence. Upon it depended, not alone his citizenship in the commonwealth, but his life itself. And shall it be deemed less real in this dispensation, when shadows have given way to substance, types to their fulfilment ? If the sanctification of the Jew was a great and practical reality, how much more the sanctification of the believer now. " If the blood of bulls and goats, and the ashes of an heifer, sprinkling the unclean, sanctifieth to the purifying of the flesh, *how much more* shall the blood of Christ purge your conscience from dead works to serve the living God ? "

And again, the practical maintenance of holiness is the true effort of a heart that grace has mastered. But yet, as with the prisoner who struggles to his window, and wipes out every stain, making it shine again, with a zeal no sense of duty could arouse, his thought is only of the sunlight he is yearning for, so is it with the soul that is alive to God. All true life leads to Him, and holiness is eagerly pursued, only to be forgotten in the enjoyment of its end and aim. Hence the exhortation and warning, " Follow holiness, *without which no man shall see the Lord*."

10

RECONCILIATION

" HAPPY art thou O Israel ! who is like unto thee, O people saved by Jehovah." Such were the last words of the blessing wherewith Moses blessed the people ere he died. " Who is like unto thee, O people saved by Jehovah ! " [1]

But if God is the Saviour of His people, He has a purpose toward them in salvation. " I bare you on eagles' wings and *brought you to Myself*," [2] was His word to Israel, and such is the great end and aim of the work of Christ to usward. God would have His people near Him. The death of Christ was " to bring us unto God." By that blood we are "made nigh." Here then is the climax of the gospel, and to stop short of this is to lose the highest blessing by separating the Giver from His gifts.

I have already treated of the doctrine of the opening chapters of the Epistle to the Romans. The great truth of righteousness by faith is there established, every objection answered, every difficulty met ; and when we reach the fifth chapter, it no longer needs even to be asserted. That we are justified by faith may now be assumed as a truth beyond question, and a fact beyond doubt, and so

[1] Deut. xxxiii. 29.　　　　[2] Ex. xix. 4.

the apostle passes on to higher teaching still. And here the first word is PEACE. " Being justified by faith, let us have peace with God." [1] Our justification is not itself our peace, nor yet the source of peace. It only clears the way which leads to it. Righteousness once barred the door against us, it now flings that door wide open. Then let us enter in. As we stood without, it was " God the Justifier " we believed in ; now we stand face to face with " God the Reconciler." We are justified through redemption in Christ, but our peace is not in redemption, but in Himself. It is not merely what He did for us, overwhelming though the record of it be, but what He is for us, and what He is to God. We have peace with God through our Lord Jesus Christ.

And here, as we stand beneath a cloudless heaven, for Christ our peace is there, we come to discern in its fulness that He Himself was the way by which we entered. By Him it is that " we have access by faith into this grace wherein we stand." [2] This grace ; not righteousness, *that* he has treated of, and he has now passed beyond it, but reconciliation, peace. Being justified, we have access through Christ into this sphere where the sunlight of God's presence is unhindered ; then let us not

---

[1] Rom. v. 1, R.V. Alford here remarks :—" It is impossible to resist the strong MS. authority for the reading ἔχωμεν in this verse," though he struggles hard against it, and pleads that " every internal consideration tends to impugn it. If admitted, the sentence is *hortatory*." I have no doubt that the sentence is hortatory, and I gladly accept the corrected reading as being thoroughly in harmony with the doctrine and purpose of the passage.

[2] Rom. v. 2.

remain without, where all is dark and cold. We have access, let us be eager to avail ourselves of it It is not an inference from what goes before, but an exhortation based upon it. And it is an exhortation, moreover, than which none is more needed with those who have the faith of the Reformation. For us the great doctrine of righteousness has been rescued in a long and deadly struggle. It has come down to us through a bitter and bloody controversy, and it is but natural that we should attach to it exceptional importance. But let us take heed lest we exalt truth at the expense of Him through whom our every blessing comes. To make one blessing a mere consequence of another, treating peace as a result of justification, is little better than pointing to a dead Christ upon a cross, and thence reasoning out salvation as a necessary consequence.

Reconciliation is a step beyond redemption even in its fulness as including both righteousness and holiness. Reconciliation is, as I have said, the fulfilment of the purpose of redemption. It is a most superficial thought, from which a right sense of what God is, or even of what we are, would save us, that forensic or even moral fitness for the presence of God gives any title to approach Him. The cross of Christ has obtained redemption for us, but more than this, it has made peace. We are not only justified and sanctified, but, as a fuller and further blessing, " we are *made nigh* by the blood of Christ, for He is our peace." [1] Not that we would tolerate the thought, more false

---

[1] Eph. ii. 13, 14.

and evil still, that God required a victim in whose blood His wrath might quench itself. The cross was Christ's work, but it was a work done for God. God is Himself the Peace-maker. It is not that Christ has reconciled us to God, but that God has reconciled us to Himself. And God *has* done this, and we have now access to it, and stand in it. I insist on this, because there is scarcely any truth so little known. It is not only that we are pardoned, and justified, and sanctified. All this was true of saints before the cross, and it is not in virtue of these blessings that we can come near to God, for if it were, there would have been access, then, as now. But not even the priests could enter the divine presence ; not even Aaron, save when, once a year on the day of atonement, in virtue of his typical office, he passed within the veil.

I do not speak here of the experience of the heart that learned of God, for there is no experience higher than the Psalms. But what was then the attainment of the few, is now the privilege of all ; what was then a secret known only to them that feared the Lord, is now a public revelation to the Church.[1] It was, then, a promise faith could grasp ; it is now no longer a promise merely, but a fact. And it is a fact for every saint who has ever lived ; but it was postponed for them of old, that they apart from us might not be made perfect.[2] It is in Christ that the believer is accepted,

[1] Ps. xxv. 14. And compare Ps. xxxiv. 2 with Rom. v. 11. " We joy (or boast) in God."

[2] Heb. xi. 40.

and in Him God is well pleased. The believer may fail to enter into this, but it is none the less a fact ; God has reconciled us to Himself, let us then know the peace of it.

But not only has the ministry of reconciliation an aspect toward the believer, and here it is too much neglected, but it is also the very essence of the gospel. Mark the words, " we *were* reconciled by the death of His Son." Righteousness is not spoken of thus. Justification is an act of God's grace toward the sinner who believes. Reconciliation is a work accomplished on the cross of Christ. It is a work done on Calvary for God and to God, apart from its consequences to the sinner altogether ; and the believer has access to it by faith through Christ as now risen from the dead. " We were reconciled through His death " ; but here is a further and higher blessing, " Through Him we have now received the reconciliation." [1] Righteousness is now the rock beneath our feet. The cloudless sky above is peace. Glory no longer threatens wrath, but fills the sinner's breast with hope. And thus the purpose of creation is accomplished through redemption, God can rejoice in the creature of His hand, and the creature can rejoice in his God.

And let us not fritter away the truth by supposing this reconciliation to mean a change in the sinner's heart to God. That is not reconciliation,

---

[1] *Not* " the atonement." The word is καταλλαγὴ. It occurs again only in Rom. xi. 15, and 2 Cor. v. 18, 19. The kindred verb is used only here (Rom. v. 10), and in 1 Cor. vii. 11, and 2 Cor. v. 18, 19, 21 ; and ἀποκαταλλάττω in Eph. ii. 16, and Col. i. 20, 21. The word in Heb. ii. 17 is different. (See chap. xvi. *post.*)

but the present work of the Holy Spirit. The change is in the attitude of God to men. Sin not only turned the creature's face from heaven, but made the sinner the enemy of God. That there is enmity to God in the sinner's breast is but too true, but it is not the truth here spoken of. It is impossible that God can be indifferent to His creature ; He must be either for him or against him ; He must regard him either with a smile or with a frown ; and sin draws down a frown, and not a smile. Apart from the work of Christ, He cannot but be against the sinner ; He reckons him an enemy. But " when we were enemies we were reconciled to God by the death of His Son." [1] " God was reconciling the world to Himself in Christ." [2] It is not a present work, but a work past and finished. By that death we who were enemies were reconciled. The appeal of the gospel is now that men would receive the reconciliation. " Be reconciled to God," [3] is not an entreaty to the sinner to forgive his God, but an appeal to him to come within the reconciliation God has wrought.

And this is the free gift of the 5th of Romans.[4] It is not righteousness, it is not life ; though it is unto righteousness, and brings life to the sinner who

---

[1] Rom. v. 10. This means either that when we were, in an active sense, enemies, we received God into our favour ; or that when we were enemies in a passive sense, He received us into His favour. Can any one doubt which is intended ? And see specially Rom. xi. 15, 28.

[2] 2 Cor. v. 19.   [3] 2 Cor. v. 20.

[4] Rom. v. 15, 16, 18. There are three words here used : χάρισμα, δωρεά, and δώρημα. The first, translated " free gift," signifies a benefit, or act of grace, or favour conferred.

receives it. It has effects as widespread as the sin of Adam. " As through one trespass the judgment came unto all men to condemnation, even so through one act of righteousness the free gift came unto all men to justification of life." [1] Not that all men are in fact made righteous, but that such was the direction and tendency of the grace. It is no question here of results to one sinner or another, but of what the Cross is to God, even though never a child of Adam should be blessed because of it. The sin of Adam turned the throne of God into a throne of judgment. The Cross of Christ has changed that throne into a throne of grace The throne of God cannot possibly be other than a throne of righteousness, but grace now reigns through righteousness. It is not that there is mercy for those who seek it, but that God's attitude to this world of ours is *grace*. Apart from the cross of Christ, righteousness could only deal forth death, and therefore sin was in fact supreme. Sin reigned: it made the very throne of God an agency for enforcing payment of its wages. But now, sin is dethroned, and " grace reigns through righteousness unto eternal life by Jesus Christ our Lord." [2]

To speak thus of the work of Christ as done to Godward, and as having an importance infinitely beyond its results upon ourselves, may perhaps seem strange to many ; and yet a due appreciation of what sin is would prepare the mind for such a truth. We are apt to think of sin only in connection with its consequences to ourselves, just as those who live in crime come to estimate it solely by its penalties. But if the effects of sin be indeed both sad and terrible, these ought rather to turn our thoughts to the essential character of sin itself. If the stream be deadly to its most distant limits, how dire must be the source from which it springs ! We do well to think upon the results of sin, but let us not lose sight of what it is which leads to these results. It makes the sinner guilty and unholy, and calls down judgment and wrath from God. But there is more in sin than this. In its essential character it is neither guilt, nor yet defilement, though both these qualities pertain to it, but *law-lessness*. " Sin is lawlessness," [1] the assertion of the creature's independence, the repudiation therefore of the Creator's supremacy, the denial of the Godhood of his Maker. Sin has " brought death into the world and all our woes " ; but more and infinitely worse than this, it has compromised the sceptre and throne of God.

I might pause here to mark how every attribute of God has thus been called in question ; not righteousness and holiness alone, but wisdom, and power, and love. Nor, for proof, should I need to pollute the page by citing what infidelity has urged about the origin of evil. I might appeal to thoughts as wicked, which, like unclean birds of night, flit about dark corners of the Christian's heart, and which only the sunlight of the gospel can drive forth. It is not that sin should go unpunished, nor yet that hell can be a doom too terrible for sinners guilty of the blood of Christ. But if sin must lead to consequences so terrible, why was the tempter's

---

[1] ἡ ἁμαρτία ἐστὶν ἡ ἀνομία. 1 John iii. 4.

whisper not restrained ? why was not the mother of our race protected from his wiles ? Nay, to go still further back, why did Lucifer himself turn Devil ? why did a good and wise and mighty God allow His noblest creature thus to fall ?

Such thoughts as these afford no proof of mental vigour or exceptional sagacity. They are one of the sad fruits of sin itself, and are shared by every child of Adam. The Christian looks off to Calvary, and awaits with patient confidence the day when all shall be made plain. But it is no mere flight of fancy, but sober truth which every thoughtful person will endorse, that, were it not for Calvary, the mystery must have remained unsolved for ever. Judgment fires might have avenged the majesty of Heaven, but the fact of a lost creation would have survived, an eternal proof that God had been thwarted in His work. Before Heaven all sin is treason ; and though rebellion be stamped out by force irresistible, it must leave a stain behind. That sin should be punished and put down is a mere matter of course with Almighty power ; but if God were indeed a God to His creatures, would He not have prevented sin altogether ? We see then that sin has effects reaching far beyond the ruin of the sinner, and gives rise to questions which the judgment of the sinner cannot settle. The Godhood of God is compromised.[1]

And as far as ever sin has reached, Christ has followed it and triumphed over it. It is but natural that our mean and selfish hearts should slight the work of Christ, save in so far as it brings blessing to

[1] See chap. xviii. *post.*

ourselves ; but its highest character and its greatest glory depend, not on what it accomplishes for men, but on what it is to God. It is no mere remedy for the ruin of our race ; it is God's answer to every question to which sin has given rise. Blessed be His name ! it has brought salvation to lost and guilty men ; but it has a purpose and a scope as wide as creation itself.

This gospel of the reconciliation " was preached in the whole creation under heaven."[1] Mankind alone can intelligently hear it, and of mankind they alone who hearken shall be blessed thereby. But in its range and compass the benefit has got no limits, and the day is coming when all this sin-cursed world shall share it. " The whole creation groans," but it shall one day be delivered from this bondage into the glorious liberty of the sons of God. Then shall all things indeed look up and put their trust in Him, and be satisfied from the fulness of His goodness. There shall be nothing more to hurt or to destroy. God will again become indeed a God to every creature He has made.[2]

But if the reconciliation be for all, how is judgment possible ? I answer, judgment is based upon this very truth. Sin is not an offence against law merely, it is an outrage upon grace. Light came into the world, but men quenched it. God has now set it on high, beyond the reach of wicked hands, and though men may hate or despise it, it shines none the less. The difficulty springs from that false view of the gospel I have already noticed,[3] which

[1] Col. 1. 23. ἐν πάσῃ κτίσει. Compare Rom. viii. 19, 22.
[2] Ps. cxlv. 15, 16. [3] See chap. vii. *ante.*

connects the sinner's blessings with the death of Christ in such a sense as to exclude the present action of the grace of God. His death has made it a righteous thing to justify ungodly sinners, and but for that death it were impossible ; and yet when the blessing reaches us, it comes direct from the hand and heart of God, and depends absolutely on sovereign grace, and on what Christ is to God as now risen from the dead.

The great end and aim of the work of Christ from first to last is to restore to God the place from which sin has struggled to dethrone Him. Its glory is that it has enabled Him to be gracious *to whom He will*, and to show mercy upon *whom He will*. It has set grace free, but it has not brought righteousness into bondage. It was first of all a work done to God-ward, and for God ; and here is at once the secret of the Christian's confidence and of his highest joy, while it is the power of the gospel to bring peace to the sinner in his sins. It is because of what GOD has found in Christ and in His cross, that the lost sinner may be saved, and the saved sinner may rejoice in hope of glory, and exult in God Himself.

Adam walked in Eden beneath an open heaven, but sin called up black clouds that covered from horizon to horizon, leaving the world in darkness. Promises and covenants, and blessing upon blessing, pierced the gloom ; and, like the Hebrew huts in Egypt, faithful hearts were filled with light from heaven while darkness reigned around.[1] And the clouds that shut out heaven were merciful. If the sunlight cannot bless and gladden, it must only

[1] Ex. x. 21-23.

scorch and wither. Judgment will be in flaming fire, with unshrouded glory, but judgment was not yet ; and God, who could not smile upon a world of sin, in mercy hid His face. Nor was judgment His purpose toward the sinner. Wrath is but a last resource with power, and judgment must wait on grace. Before God will declare Himself to be the Judge, He must reveal Himself as RECONCILER.

Judgment is still to come; but reconciliation is accomplished. Now, God need hide His face no longer. An opened heaven will disclose a throne of grace, where the guiltiest sinner may draw nigh. The work of Christ has banished every cloud, and swept our sky as clear as when Adam walked in innocence with God. The light of this glorious gospel now shines unhindered upon earth. Blind eyes may shut it out, but they cannot quench or lessen it. Impenitent hearts may heap up wrath against the day of wrath, but they cannot darken this day of mercy or mar the glory of the reign of grace.

But though we have reached the summit of this vast and glorious truth in its bearings upon Adam and his world, the Scripture points us higher still. And yet we may not follow. The height is too stupendous ; and if we gaze with reverence and awe, it is that thereby we may shake free from the littlenesses of our poor and niggard hearts, and gain truer thoughts of our glorious Lord. The words I have quoted from the Epistle to the Colossians are the sequel to a passage which is one of the most sublime in Holy Writ. The Gnostic philosophy, which made such havoc in the early Church, was gaining ground among the Christians of Colosse. Oriental theories of the creation of the world, the origin of evil, and the intrinsic corruptness of everything corporeal, were undermining the faith of Christ. The Son was thus degraded to the position of a creature, while yet the reality of " the body of His flesh " was set aside. Inferior beings were made the agents in our creation, thus gaining a title to our homage, and the Godhood of God was practically denied. But He who can " bring meat out of the eater, and honey out of the strong," has made these evils and errors the occasion of the fullest and most glorious revelation to the Church, of Him before whom we bow as Lord.[1]

Christ is, indeed, the First-born of all creation, yet not because He has His place within it. If He holds this title of dignity and precedence relatively to the universe, it is because it exists as His creature. The whole universe,—things in the heavens and things in the earth, things visible and invisible, whether thrones, or dominions, or principalities, or powers,—all things have been created by Him, and for Him. He was the One who called them into being, and He is the end and aim of their existence. And He Himself exists before all things, and it is in virtue of His power that the universe subsists   And He is the Head of the body, the Church, in that He

---

[1] Col. i. 15–20, v. 15, all creation, *not* every creature ; v. 16, ἐν αὐτῷ, not merely that He was the agent in creation—that is expressed afterwards in δι' αὐτοῦ, but that the universe is His creature. τὰ πάντα, " the universe." " Thus only can we give the force of the Greek singular with the collective neuter plural " (Alford). Compare Eph. i. 21, and 1 Cor. xv. 24, 27. Verse 17, ἐν αὐτῷ, as in v. 16 : v. 19, compare chap. ii. 9 : v. 20, " the universe," as in v. 16.

is the beginning, the First-born from among the dead, that He may become in all things pre-eminent. And God was pleased that the whole fulness should dwell in Him. And He was pleased by Him to reconcile again the universe to Himself, having made peace by the blood of His cross ; by Him, whether the things on the earth or the things in the heavens—the creation of God in every part and to its utmost limits.[1]

In the presence of words so plain and simple, faith will not dare to question or to doubt ; and in view of truth so immeasurably vast and deep, no worshipping heart will venture upon argument or inference. " Secret things belong to the Lord our

[1] A valued and revered friend, to whose judgment these latter chapters have been submitted, suggests to me that Revelation xxi. gives the complete fulfilment of the reconciliation spoken of in Colossians i. The thought is full of interest. It is certain that millennial blessedness and glory will be a direct result and proof of the preciousness of the cross of Christ to God ; but it is no less certain that an eternity of glory and blessedness, still to follow, will depend upon that cross as really and immediately. In our view, creation limits itself to our own race and sphere, but with God the universe is one great whole, of which the Adamic world is but a part. And as sin has disturbed the harmony of creation in this its widest sense, God's answer and remedy are the cross of Christ and a new creation. It is not merely the kingdoms of this world that are given up to Christ, but the throne of the universe of God. And when "the end " shall come, and God shall again assume the sceptre He will hold it in virtue of Calvary. If one could dare to speak thus of God, we might say that His moral right to make all things new depends on that blood. And the word is " I make ALL THINGS new." The promise is not of a new earth only, but of new heavens too. And why " new heavens," if sin and the cross concern only earth ? " It is finished " was the cry that rose amid the agonies of Calvary : " Behold I make all things new " is the response from the glory. The " It is finished " of the cross, shall still vibrate until it is lost in the " It is done " of the throne. (Rev. xxi. 5, 6.)

God," and it is not given us to know what the death of Christ may bring to other worlds than ours. But " things which are revealed belong to us and to our children," and this at least is plain as God can make it, that that death shall bring either eternal life, or judgment, to every child of Adam to whom the gospel testimony comes. Men may reason of the Fatherhood of God, and idly dream of universal blessing, or at least of the annihilation of the lost ; and none would rejoice as would the Christian, if such might be the end of wicked men. But to construe Scripture thus is in fact to slip the anchor of our hope of life eternal ; for it is in the very words which promise blessing that God has warned of wrath. " These shall go away into *everlasting* punishment, but the righteous into *everlasting* life." [1]

[1] The Christian maintains that the punishment of the lost will be everlasting, not because he *wishes* it to be so, but because he *believes* it to be so. The objection that it *cannot* be everlasting is either a puerility or a denial of the supremacy of God. The objection that the words which express the duration of it do not, in ordinary or classical Greek, mean really "everlasting," is a mere quibble. What other words in the language would serve to convey the idea at all, assuming it existed ? The fact is that no language which is not based upon Christianity could possess such a word, for, apart from Christianity, no one ever conceived such a thought. Plato comes nearer it than any one else among the heathen ; but Revelation alone pretends to speak of an eternity beyond " the end " (1 Cor. xv. 24). The only clew to the meaning of a word in the dead languages is the use of it ; and if " everlasting life " means a life which shall have no limit to its duration, it is wanton to construe " everlasting punishment " on a different principle. I may add that every objection of any weight which has been urged against eternal punishment, applies as really, though not to the same extent, to punishment for a millennium or a century. And if the Christian be wrong, no one will suffer from his error ; but if he is right, how terrible must be the discovery for those who

The day is near in which God Himself shall be the only mystery unsolved ; when faith and hope shall merge in the completeness of our knowledge, and the realisation of every promise that has cheered us here. But faith and hope are now the guide and beacon of our life, and we hail this unfathomable mystery of reconciliation as placing yet another crown upon our Saviour's brow. Upon His head are *many* crowns, but His pierced hand now holds the only sceptre , for the Father has given Him the kingdom, and all things are placed beneath His feet. The outcast of the earth now fills the throne of God.

" We *see* not yet all things put under Him," for a long-suffering God still waits, and grace must spend itself ere judgment can sweep back on those whom grace has failed to win. But we do see Jesus, the rejected and despised of men, now crowned with glory. He is the mighty God, the Father of Eternity, the Prince of Peace, and the government is on His shoulder, and all power is His in heaven and on earth. And He it is who is our Saviour, and through Him the weakest and the worst of men may gain deliverance from judgment and from sin. Willing knees now bow before Him, and willing hearts confess His name ; but the day is hastening on when every knee, in heaven, earth, and hell, *shall* bow, and every tongue shall own Him Lord.[1]

" And then THE END, when He shall have de-

---

trade upon the hope that he is wrong ! In my *Human Destiny* I have dealt with this whole subject, discussing and refuting both the heresy of annihilation and that of universal restoration.

[1] Phil. ii. 9-11

livered up the kingdom to God, even the Father ; when He shall have put down all rule and all authority and power. For He must reign, till He hath put all enemies under His feet. And when all things shall be subdued unto Him, then shall the Son also Himself be subject unto Him that put all things under Him, that God may be all in all." [1]

Such then is the Christian's faith, and such his hope : no day-dream of weak minds, no fable cunningly devised, but a hope both sure and steadfast, and a most holy faith. A vain philosophy may reason of the past, and dream about the future, but, in the calm confidence of faith, the Christian can look back to a past eternity, when, before all time, and ere there was a creature made, " IN THE BEGINNING " the Word was alone with God ; and on through the ages of ages to " THE END," when, time having run its course, in the midst of His creation, God shall be all in all : and in adoration he exclaims, " From everlasting to everlasting Thou art God ! "

[1] 1 Cor. xv. 24, 25, and 28.

11

JUSTIFICATION BY FAITH

JUSTIFICATION by faith is a divine truth ; and yet every thoughtful person revolts against the idea that eternal blessedness depends upon apprehending aright a formula or creed respecting Christ, or upon assenting to certain facts concerning Him. No one represents this to be the doctrine of Holy Scripture, save those who do so in order to discredit it. But there are many who, though in a sense lovers of truth, suppose this to be the view of evangelical Christians, and who, in rejecting it, reject also the teaching of Scripture respecting faith. To such, therefore, a plain statement is due of what in fact we deem to be the truth in this matter. And I venture to think, moreover, that among Christians generally there exists a great deal of confusion of thought, and somewhat of error too, with respect to it. The gospel will bear the test of the severest metaphysical inquiry, but it is addressed to plain people, and not to metaphysicians ; and we may be certain that the doctrine of faith is not a subtle difficulty, but a truth within the reach of all.

Now, as I have sought to show, the attempt to solve the question by declaring *trust* to be the true

and only faith recognised by God is utterly wrong.[1]
Trust is a fruit of faith in its simplest phase, but not
necessarily a part of it. Suppose in a money panic
I am in fear of ruin, and I receive a letter telling me
that the bank in which my fortune is invested is
absolutely safe, it is faith of the simplest kind to
believe that testimony ; and, simply believing it, I
dismiss my fears. But, it will be answered, such
faith, simple though it be, depends entirely on the
confidence I repose in my informant. Undoubtedly
it does. The words of the letter, as it lies before me,
are like counters that may stand for anything or
nothing. These counters become gold in my estimation, because I import into them the element of
pre-existing trust in the writer. It is clear then
that, between man and man, faith, apart from proof,
assumes trust, and is inseparable from it.

But is this true also as between God and the
sinner ? Believing the Bible as a book merely, or
even as a book recognised as true, is no doubt
governed by the same principle. But when God
speaks to the soul, His message is a living word, a
word of power, and that quite independently of
evidences, or of the condition of the hearer, It
finds the sinner morally incapable of trust in God,
for the essence of his nature is distrust of Him—
" the carnal mind is enmity against God." And
spiritually he is no less incapable of trust, for he is
spiritually dead. But the gospel itself brings life to
the dead soul, and masters the enmity of the carnal
heart. It brought forth fruit among the Colossians;
" *from the day they heard it.*" [2] By nature man is

[1] See chap. iv. *ante.*   [2] Col. i. 6.

fallen and apostate, and the gospel is itself the instrument for his recovery and conversion ; in no sense, therefore, and in no degree, does it rely for its acceptance upon any pre-existing quality or condition of heart.

In speaking thus, however, we must guard against the folly of supposing that any set of words in Greek or Hebrew, or their more or less accurate counterparts in English, have inherent power or virtue to bring salvation to the person who believes them. And if the words themselves can work no charm, the belief of them will not help the matter. Nor can we consent to fall back upon distinctions between " faith about Christ " and " faith in (or on) Christ," as is sometimes done—distinctions which pertain either to language or to metaphysics. The one question is interesting, and I will deal with it for any who have leisure and inclination to follow me ; but the metaphysical inquiry I must decline to enter on here. For, as I have said, the gospel is for those who are incapable of such a study ; and, moreover, the distinction is based upon the assumption that, of the various " sorts of faith " (to use a popular expression), one is efficacious, and the other not ; thus attaching merit to faith itself, and coming under the almost ironical remonstrance of the Apostle James, " Can *faith* save ? "

If by " faith about Christ " be meant the belief of facts concerning Him, to say that in Scripture this is not connected with salvation is a statement so glaringly false as to need no answer. It is certainly inadequate as a definition of the true faith of the gospel, as I will presently explain ; but changing the preposition will in no way supply the defect. The distinction assumes that the form of words translated in the Authorised Version " to believe *in* " (or *on*) implies trust in the person who is the object of the faith. But this is quite untenable. In saying I believe in any one, I may mean that I thoroughly rely upon him, or I may merely intend that I acknowledge him to be the person he claims to be. Every one will admit that the expression has this elasticity of meaning in our own language ; and it needs no scholarship to ascertain for oneself that it has equal scope in Greek, and notably in the writings of the Apostle John.[1]

Having thus cleared the ground of difficulties and distinctions which are both irrelevant and unworthy of the subject, I fall back upon the main inquiry, What is the element which connects faith with salvation ?

[1] The fact is that the difference between π. εἰς τινα and π. τινι is purely a matter of etymology or of style ; and in every case the force of the words depends entirely upon the context. John uses them convertibly. See, for instance, John viii. 30, 31, where both are rightly translated " believed on Him," *i.e.*, gave in their adhesion to His Messiahship. The 29th and 30th verses of chap. vi. afford another example. And again compare 1 John iii. 23 (π. τῷ ὀνόματι) with v. 13 (π. εἰς τὸ ὄνομα). Moreover, in John v. 24, Acts xvi. 34, xviii. 8, Rom. iv. 3, and elsewhere, the verb without the preposition denotes " saving faith " beyond all question ; and in numerous passages π. εἰς is used where as plainly there is no thought of either salvation or trust. I would include John viii. 30, already quoted, in this category, as the context plainly demands ; but such passages as vii. 48, xi. 48, are unequivocal instances of it. π. ἐπί does seem to include the idea of confidence or trust , but this is used but seldom, and never by John, though the word *believe* occurs in his writings well nigh as often as in all the rest of the New Testament. π. ἐπί occurs Luke xxiv. 25 ; Acts ix. 42, xi. 17, xvi. 31, xxii. 19 ; Rom. iv. 5, 24, ix.₀33, x. 11 ; 1 Pet. ii. 6.

It is not owing to any virtue or charm in the text of the message received, nor does it depend on any merit or vitality in faith, in what sense soever faith be understood. Still less is it to be accounted for by some fitness or worth in the recipient. If then it depends neither upon the message, nor yet upon the faith, nor upon the character of the faith, nor upon the condition of him who exercises the faith, there is but one more alternative remaining. And here, as the result of a circuitous inquiry, we reach once more a conclusion which every true believer will enthusiastically accept. It is not that the sinner *believes*, nor yet that he believes the *gospel*, but that he believes GOD. The belief of the facts of Christianity, however great and true, or even of the inspired record of them, can never bring life to a dead soul, or change a sinner's destiny. But that which makes the gospel a word of power and life to some, and links blessing with the faith of it, is that to such it comes as a divine voice by the Holy Ghost now present upon earth to that end. " Faith cometh by hearing, and hearing by the Word of God " ; not by the Bible as a volume purchased at a book shop, but by those sacred words when through them a present God speaks to the soul.

If it be objected that this is transcendentalism, the ready answer is that it is *Christianity*. Grace is boundless, but it is *sovereign* ; and if God has brought salvation within the reach of all, it is not by making men independent of Himself, but by giving the Holy Ghost to bear witness to the finished work and glorified person of a Saviour. In apostolic days, the gospel was preached " with the Holy Ghost sent down from heaven," and this is still its only power.   It is not as a true record merely, but as a living word from God, that it is indeed " the power of God unto salvation to every one that believeth."

12

JUSTIFICATION BY WORKS

" WAS not Abraham our father justified by works when he had offered Isaac his son upon the altar ? Thou seest how faith wrought with his works, and by works faith was made perfect.

" And so," says many a one, closing the book, " we see how the Scripture which says ' Abraham believed God, and it was imputed unto him for righteousness,' is guarded and explained."

" And so," continues the Apostle James, " the Scripture *was fulfilled*, which saith, Abraham believed God, and it was imputed unto him for righteousness, and he was called the friend of God." [1]

Justification by works, as an article of man's religion, is opposed to justification by faith, and therefore it denies the grace of God, and dishonours the blood of Christ. Justification by works, according to the Epistle of James, is the complement, so to speak, of justification by faith. It owns grace, and does homage to the blood.

But " it is of faith that it may be by *grace* " ; and grace puts works, and merit in every phase of it, out of court altogether. What then if a man regard his faith as a meritorious thing ? He thereby

[1] Jas. ii. 14–26.

denies grace entirely. He makes a saviour of his own faith ; and " can faith save him ? " It is no longer a question between God's grace on the one side, and the sinner's merit on the other ; but merely a rivalry between faith and works. The Epistle to the Romans is essentially doctrinal, and the practical is based upon the doctrine. The Epistle " to the twelve tribes scattered abroad," is essentially practical, the doctrinal element being purely incidental. Paul's Epistle unfolds the mind and purposes of God, revealing His righteousness and wrath. The Epistle of James addresses men upon their own ground. The one deals with justification as between the sinner and God, the other as between man and man. In the one, therefore, the word is, " To him that *worketh not*, but believeth." In the other it is, " What is the profit if a man say he hath faith, and have not works ? " Not " If a man have faith," but " If a man *say* he hath faith " ; proving that, in the case supposed, the individual is not dealing with God, but arguing the matter with his brethren. God, who searches the heart, does not need to judge by works, which are but the outward manifestation of faith within ; but man can judge only by appearances.

Faith identifies a sinner with a Saviour God. But it is nothing in itself. A man cannot show another his faith, any more than he can show him his charity. One who says he has faith, but whose conduct is not that of a believer, is like a man who says he has charity, but does no charitable actions ; who dismisses a starving beggar with kind words and nothing more. " Even so," says the Epistle, just in the same sense, " faith, if it hath not works, is dead, being alone." You believe in one God. Well, quite right : so do the devils ; and what comes of it ? They tremble, and so ought you. Believing cannot, therefore, be in itself a meritorious thing. But if it be indeed, to use a favourite metaphor, a laying hold of God, it will declare itself by results. Abraham's case is an instance. He believed God, and it was imputed unto him for righteousness. That is, Abraham believed and God blessed him, " He was holden for righteous, in virtue of faith." Well, the result was that Abraham acted. God discerned the faith ; man judged of the acts. He believed, and God declared he was righteous. He acted, and man acknowledged he was righteous. He was justified by faith when judged by God, for God knows the heart. He was justified by works when judged by his fellow-men ; for man can only read the life. And just as faith is made perfect, or fulfilled, by works, so the Scripture which says " He was justified by faith," is made perfect, or fulfilled, by the declaration, " He was justified by works."

So then, though in one sense a man is justified by faith without works, in another sense we see " how by works a man is justified, and not by faith only." Justified by faith before God ; justified by works before men. This is not mere assertion ; nor is it a plausible piece of sophistry. It is not only that these Scriptures admit of no other explanation, but that this explanation is thoroughly in keeping with the respective characters of the two epistles. And, moreover, just as in the 23rd verse, the Apostle

James guards the truth of justification by faith ; so, in the Epistle to the Romans, the Apostle Paul alludes to the aspect of the truth here insisted on—" If Abraham were justified by works," he declares, " he hath whereof to glory, *but not before God.*" [1]

[1] Rom. iv. 2.

13

JUSTIFICATION BY BLOOD

JUDICIAL righteousness is theoretically possible in either of two ways. The law-keeper is righteous as such; the law-breaker may become righteous through redemption. The law-keeper fulfils the demands of the law by his obedience; the law-breaker may fulfil the demands of the law by enduring to the full its penalties in the person of Christ. Righteousness on the first ground is shown to be in fact impossible, and it is set aside altogether. The sinner is therefore shut up to "justification by blood." Vicarious obedience is an idea wholly beyond reason; how could a God of righteousness and truth reckon a law-breaker to have kept the law, because some one else has kept it? The thief is not declared to be honest because his neighbour or his kinsman is a good citizen. Punishment may be remitted on this ground, but that is not justification. The merits of ten righteous men would have saved Sodom, but God would not therefore have called Sodom righteous.

But is not the thought of vicarious judgment as much beyond reason as vicarious obedience? Possibly it is. But to accept what is above our reason is the very highest exercise of reason if revelation testifies to it—otherwise it is mere superstition ; whereas the bearing of judgment in the person of a substitute is a foundation truth of Christianity. Obedience by a substitute is a mere theory, and one of the strangest in the entire range of human thought. It is the Protestant version of the Roman Catholic heresy of the imputation of the merits of the saints ; and both versions deny the great truth of Christianity, that the believing sinner is justified through redemption, apart from law altogether.[1]

One poem may not constitute a man a poet, but one murder makes a man a murderer, one sin makes a sinner. Nothing but the gallows can expiate a murder ; death alone can atone for sin. The law is a standard, so to speak, to which man is subjected —not his acts merely, but himself. If he comes up to it, he is thereby justified, justified by law. If he fails, he is thereby condemned, and law can never justify him ; for a law that could justify an offender would be an immoral and corrupt law. The law has pronounced its sentence, and nothing remains but the fulfilment of that sentence. This is the natural state of the sinner under law. But here God reveals himself a Saviour. He gives up His Only-begotten Son to take the place of the condemned sinner, and die in his stead. He now points to that death as satisfying the righteous demand of law against the sinner, and on that ground He justifies him. Not that by virtue of His sovereignty, or by a legal fiction, as we say, He reckons the believer to be righteous while leaving

[1] See chap. vii. *ante*, and especially pp. 108–109.

his condition in fact unchanged, but that He *justifies* him. The believer is "justified from all things from which he could not be justified by the law of Moses." [1] God imputes the death of Christ to the believer.

If it be demanded, How can this be ? I answer it depends upon the fact that God imputed the sin of the believer to Christ, and that He died under sin and for sin. Not that the guiltless died as guiltless for the guilty, which would be horrible ; but that the guiltless passed into the position of the guilty, and as guilty died to expiate the guilt imputed to Him : " He who knew no sin was made sin for us." If the inquiry be still further pressed, and the question be insisted on, How could sin be so imputed to the sinless as to make a vicarious death justifiable ? men may seek to reason out the answer, but, as Bishop Butler says, " All conjectures about it must be, if not evidently absurd, yet at least uncertain." " Nor," he adds, " has he any reason to complain from want of further information, unless he can show his claim to it." Here it is that God retreats upon His own sovereignty, and the believer is satisfied with the divine " It is written." Reason bows before the God of reason, and the reasoner becomes a disciple and a worshipper.

Moreover, though the revelation of the death of Christ as a sin-bearer is indeed a great mystery, it is by no means so incredible as would be the story of His death apart from sin. The thorough infidel is consistent in his unbelief, and the true Christian in his faith ; but the most utterly unreasonable

[1] Acts xiii. 39.

person in the world is the man who accepts the *fact* of the death of Christ the Lord of life and glory, and yet doubts whether it was a death for sin. That Jesus of Nazareth died upon a cross is mere matter of history ; that He who did so die was the Christ the Son of God is entirely a matter of revelation. And the seeming impossibility of the gospel is the stupendous fact that Christ has died, not that that death was because of sin, nor yet that the sinner can be blessed in virtue of it.[1]

The 18th and 19th verses of the 5th of Romans are sometimes quoted in support of the doctrine of vicarious obedience, but wrongly so. The word in verse 18 is not " the righteousness of one," as given in the Authorised Version, but δι' ἑνὸς δικαιώματος. " By means of one righteous act—the death of Christ viewed as the acme of His obedience. See Philippians ii. 8." I quote from Dean Alford, who rightly explains " the obedience of one " in verse 19 upon the same principle   Christ was obedient unto death, and by means of that obedience we are justified—" justified by His blood," as the apostle had already asserted in the 9th verse, and explained in the earlier chapters of the Epistle.[2]

[1] See chap. iii. *ante.*

[2] The word δικαίωμα occurs also in the 16th verse, where it means " a righteous sentence of acquittal." In i. 32, the same word stands for " the righteous judgment " of God ; and in ii. 26, in the plural, for " the righteous requirements " of the law. The only other passage in Romans where it is used is viii. 4. " The law of sin and death "—the active principle of sin within—made it impossible for God's law to obtain its demand from man. But the death of Christ redeemed them that were under the law ; and " the law of the Spirit of life in Christ Jesus " now frees them practically from " the law of sin and death." It is an active

principle of power within them, resulting in a walk after the Spirit, and not after the flesh. And thus the law receives its δικαίωμα, whereas it utterly failed of that, so long as the believer was under it.

Everywhere else in the Epistle, the word translated righteousness is δικαιοσύνη. Δικαίωσις occurs in iv. 25, and v. 18. The gift was by one δικαίωμα unto δικαίωσις.

14

HOLINESS AND SANCTIFICATION

WORDS mean exactly what they pass current for, and with the English Bible before us it is idle to insist on a distinction between " holiness " and " sanctification." But an examination of the various passages where the Greek correlatives of these terms occur will help much toward accuracy of thought and a clear grasp of the truth upon this subject.

The meaning of ἁγιάζειν (*hagiazein*) in Scripture (and I am not aware that it ever has any other meaning), is to separate, or set apart, for God, or to some sacred purpose ; and ἁγιασμός (*hagiasmos*) means either the act of consecration, or the condition into which that act introduces the subject of it. There is no question of any change of essential qualities. The subject may be (*a*) intrinsically holy already, or (*b*) it may be, and continue to be, intrinsically unholy, or (*c*) it may be incapable of moral qualities altogether. For example (*a*) Christ was sanctified by the Father,[1] (*b*) the sinner is sanctified on believing ;[2] and an unconverted husband or wife is sanctified in virtue of marriage with a holy person ;[3] and (*c*) the vessels of the temple were

[1] John x. 36.   [2] 1 Cor. vi. 11.   [3] 1 Cor. vii. 14.

sanctified, as also the creatures we use for food are " sanctified by the word of God and prayer." [1]

The word means, therefore, to make a person or thing holy, in the sense in which to justify a person is to make that person righteous. His condition is changed, but not necessarily his character. In the Appendix I give a list of all the passages where the word occurs,[2] and a careful perusal of them will show that in one case only does the word seem to bear a different meaning. I allude to the prayer of 1 Thessalonians v. 23. " The God of peace sanctify you wholly." But a consideration of the context will show that " wholly " refers not to progressive sanctification of the whole man regarded as a unit, but to the absolute sanctification of every part of the man considered as a complex being, made up of body, soul, and spirit.[3] In John xvii. it is quite unjustifiable to put a different meaning on the word " sanctify," when the Lord uses it of Himself, and when He applies it to His disciples. And Ephesians v. 26 teaches that He gave Himself for the Church " that He might sanctify it, cleansing it by the washing of water by the Word." [4]

It will be observed that we are said to be sancti-

[1] 1 Tim. iv. 4, 5.　　　　　　[2] See Appendix, Note II.

[3] So Alford and other commentators take it.

[4] Literally " having cleansed it." But these aorists may be either coincident or consequent one on another. In either case definite acts and not gradual operations are implied. The word " washing " is λουτρόν (used again in Tit. iii. 5), which is not the LXX. word for *laver*, but is used in Ecclesiasticus xxxiv. 25, for the vessel which held the water of purification (Num. xix. 18; Ezek. xxxvi. 25). The reference, of course, is not to baptism, but to the sin-offering of Numbers xix.

fied by God the Father, sanctified by the Spirit, sanctified in the name of the Lord Jesus, sanctified in Christ Jesus, and sanctified by blood. These all refer to one and the same sanctification. God is the Author, the Spirit the Agent, and the blood the means, of our sanctification, and it is in Christ that all this is ours. The attempt of some commentators to cut up verse eleven of 1st Corinthians vi., and to make "justified" refer to Christ, and "sanctified" to the Spirit, is mere special pleading. The believer is sanctified absolutely and for ever, even as he is justified ; and of necessity it is by the Spirit, for through Him it is that every blessing flows to us.

All this is confirmed by a careful study of the passages where ἁγιασμός (hagiasmos) is used. It is very remarkable that when sanctification is spoken of as by the Spirit it is connected with election, and precedes faith.[1] And the reason of this seems to be that, though chronologically faith and sanctification are simultaneous, there is nevertheless a moral order, varying according as we view the subject from our own standpoint, or from that of the sovereignty of God. In the former case, faith comes first, and sanctification follows as a consequence ; but when election comes in, we see our faith to be the result of the divine decree which *set us apart* to eternal life.

It is further remarkable that, save as above noticed, sanctification is never spoken of as being specially the work of the Spirit. But the reason of this is clear ; the truth is too obvious to need even

[1] 1 Pet. i. 2.

to be stated. It is only by the help of the Holy Spirit that a believer can stand for a moment. Truth is emphasised in Scripture, not, as in a creed, according to its doctrinal importance relatively to other truths, but according to the practical need which exists for enforcing it upon the believer.

Holiness means, as we have seen, not merely the state of being sanctified, but also the moral character akin to that state. And here the Greek, a language rich in such distinctions, is not confined to a single word. The quality or attribute of holiness is expressed by ἁγιωσύνη (*hagiōsunee*), a word, which, strange to say, is used but thrice, namely, Romans i. 4, " the Spirit of holiness " ; not the Holy Ghost, but the Spirit of Christ, in contrast with the flesh mentioned in the preceding verse ; 2 Corinthians vii. 1, upon which I have already commented ;[1] and 1 Thessalonians iii. 13, " unblameable in holiness," a very solemn and significant word, especially in the connection where it occurs. The kindred word ἁγιότης (*hagiotees*) is found only in Hebrews xii. 10, " That we might be partakers of His holiness." And ὁσιότης (*hosiotees*) in Luke i. 75 ; and Ephesians iv. 24.

A comparison of Ephesians iv. 24 with 1 Corinthians i. 30, will give an insight into the difference between this last word and ἁγιασμός (*hagiasmos*). Israel's sanctification, and indeed their entire position as a redeemed people, was maintained by the " middle wall of partition " which separated them from other nations.[2] But Christ Himself is to His people, now, what the " middle wall of partition " was to the Jew . *He* is our sanctification. The words are plain and simple : " But of Him are ye in Christ Jesus who was made unto us wisdom from God, and both righteousness and sanctification, even redemption." [1] It is only in virtue of what Christ has done for us that we can gain the place we hold in redemption : it is entirely in virtue of what Christ now is to us that we can be maintained in that place.

But in Ephesians iv. 24, it is not a question of what Christ is to us, but of the essential qualities of the new creation of which He is the Head, and of what we ourselves ought to be in practical conformity therewith. The new man is *created in holiness*. To ignore the truth that Christ is made unto us sanctification and that therefore the believer is holy, independently of his life on earth, is to abandon or deny the true position of the Christian ; but to suppose that Christ is made unto us holiness in this further sense also, would lead to the still deeper error of supposing that holy living is of no account.

[1] Both A.V. and R.V. ignore the τε καὶ of 1 Cor. i. 30. It ought of course to be rendered " both " (as in *v*. 24). And equally of course the last καί has the force of " even," for redemption includes both righteousness and sanctification.

15

CLEANSED BY BLOOD

CLEANSING with blood is a common expression in the book of Leviticus, but in the New Testament it is found only in the 9th chapter of Hebrews, and the beginning of the First Epistle of John.[1] Of Hebrews I have already spoken ;[2] but the other passage claims notice, not only because of its connection with the present subject, but also on account of the difficulties that seem to surround it :—" If we walk in the light, as He is in the light, we have fellowship one with another, and the blood of Jesus Christ His Son cleanseth us from all sin."

It is a canon of interpretation that whenever the benefits or results of the death of Christ are ascribed to His blood, the figure thus implied is borrowed from the types. It behoves us, therefore, to turn back to the Old Testament, and there to seek out the particular key-picture to which it is intended to direct our minds. In 1 Peter i., for example, the second verse will naturally turn our thoughts to the only occasion on which blood was *sprinkled* on the people of Israel (Exodus xxiv.) ; while verse 19

[1] Heb. ix. 14, 22, 23, where, as in 1 John i. 7, the word is καθαρίζω.
[2] See chap. ix. *ante.*

brings us back to their one great *redemption* sacrifice of the passover in Egypt.

Here then we have a certain clew to the meaning of the text before us : " The blood of Jesus cleanseth us from all sin." The particular type in the light of which we are to understand the word must be that of some offering which was for *sin*; and one moreover which was for the people generally, as distinguished from those which were for individuals; and further, it must be a sacrifice of which the benefits were abiding. This at once excludes all the offerings of the first fifteen chapters of Leviticus, and it will confine our consideration to the great day of expiation, prescribed in the 16th chapter. " For on that day " (was the word to Moses) " he shall make an atonement for you to cleanse you, that ye may be clean from all your sins before the Lord."[1]

We can picture to ourselves some devout Israelite telling of his God to a heathen stranger, recounting to him the proofs of Jehovah's goodness and faithfulness to His people, and going on to speak of His holiness, His terribleness—how He was " of purer eyes than to behold iniquity," and how, for acts in which his guest would fail to see sin at all, He had visited them with signal judgments. And we can conceive that, in amazement, the stranger might demand whether the people were free from the weaknesses and wickedness of other men. And, on his hearing an eager repudiation of all such pretensions, with what deepening wonder and awe he would exclaim, " How then can you live before a God so great and terrible ? "

[1] Lev. xvi. 30.

And here the heathen stranger within the gates of the Israelite, would have reached a point analogous to that to which the opening verses of John's Epistle lead us. Eternal life has been *manifested*, and life is the only ground of fellowship with God. But " God is light," and it is only in the light, as the sphere of its enjoyment, that such fellowship is possible. The light of God, how can sinners bear it ? Is it by attaining sinlessness ? The thought is proof of self-deception and utter absence of the truth (*v.* 8). But just as the question of his guest would turn the thoughts of the Israelite to his great day of expiation, and call to his lips the words, " It is the cleansing blood which alone enables us to live before Jehovah," so the Christian turns to the great Sin-offering, and his faith finds utterance in the words, " The blood of Jesus Christ His Son cleanseth us from all sin."

It is not " has cleansed," nor yet " will cleanse," but " *cleanseth.*" It is not the statement of a fact merely, but of a truth, and truths are greater and deeper even than facts.

But how " cleanseth " ?[1] Just as the blood of

[1] " *Washing* with blood " is an expression wholly unknown to the law, and it conveys an idea which is quite at variance with its teaching. It has no scriptural warrant. For the correct reading of Rev. i. 5, as given in R.V., is " Unto Him that loveth us and loosed us from our sins by His own blood." Ps. li. 7, must of course be explained by the law ; and the student of Scripture will naturally turn to the 19th of Numbers, or to Leviticus xiv. 6–9, to seek its meaning. A like remark applies to other similar passages in the Old Testament. Overlooking this, Cowper derived his extraordinary idea of a *fountain* of blood from the 13th of Zechariah, construed in connection with the received reading of Rev. i 5. The fact is that though cleansing with water was one of the most frequent and characteristic of the typical ordinances, it has been

the sin-offering cleansed the Israelite. It was not by any renewal of its application to him, but by the continuance of its efficacy. With Israel its virtue continued throughout the year ; with us it is for ever. It is not mere acts of sin that are in question here, but the deeper problem of our condition as sinners (compare *v.* 10 with *v.* 8). And neither the difficulty, nor yet the answer to it, is the same. In regard to the one the Israelite turned to the day of atonement, and said " the blood cleanseth " ; but in case of his committing some act of sin, he had to bring his sin-offering, according to the 4th or 5th or 6th chapter of Leviticus. But the need of these special offerings depended on " the weakness and unprofitableness " of the sacrifices of the old Covenant.[1] And 1 John i. 7, 9, seems clearly to teach that all our need is met by the twofold cleansing typified by the blood of the great sin-offering of

almost entirely forgotten in our creeds. " In that day there shall be a fountain opened to the house of David and to the inhabitants of Jerusalem, for sin and for separation for uncleanness." (Zech. xiii. 1, see marginal reading, and compare Num. xix. 9.) " *In that day* "—the epoch referred to in verses 9–14 of the preceding chapter —Israel shall be admitted to the full benefits of the great sin-offering typified in the 19th of Numbers. (See also Rom. xi. 25–29.) The washing of garments in blood is likewise wholly unscriptural, save in poetical language—as, *e.g.*, Genesis xlix. 11. The meaning of Revelation vii. 14 is too often frittered away thus as though it were a merely poetical expression. But the figures used are typical, not poetical : " These are they that come out of the great tribulation [compare Matt. xxiv. 21], and they washed their robes [compare Rev. xix. 8], and made them white by [ἐν] the blood of the Lamb." Their lives were purified practically from the defilements that surrounded them, and purged in a still deeper sense by the blood. In Rev. xxii. 14, also, the true reading is " Blessed are they that wash their robes."

[1] Heb. x. 9–18. See pp 126, 129 note, and 132 note *ante*.

Leviticus xvi., and the water of the great rite of Numbers xix. For the believer who sins against God to dismiss the matter by " the blood cleanseth," is the levity and daring of antinomianism. For such the word is, "*If we confess our sins*" : no flippant acknowledgment with the lip, but a solemn and real dealing with God ; and thus he obtains again and again a renewal of the benefits of the death of Christ. " He is faithful and just to forgive us our sins and to cleanse us from all unrighteousness."

And this, no doubt, is the truth intended by the popular expression " coming back to blood." The Israelite " came back to blood " by seeking a fresh sacrifice ; but had he attempted to " come back to blood " in the sense of preserving the blood of the sin-offering in order to avail himself of it for future cleansing, he would have been cut off without mercy for presumptuous sin. The most superficial knowledge either of the precepts or the principles of the book of Leviticus, will make us avoid a form of words so utterly opposed to both.

With one great exception the blood of every sin-offering was poured round the altar of burnt-offering, and thus consumed ; and that exception was the sacrifice of the 19th of Numbers, so often referred to in these pages. The red heifer was the sin-offering in that aspect of it in which the sinner can come back to it to obtain cleansing. And here the whole beast *and its blood* was burnt to ashes outside the camp, and the unclean person was cleansed by being sprinkled with water which had touched those ashes. But to confound the cleansing by blood—the 16th of Leviticus aspect of the sin-offering, with the cleansing by water—the 19th of Numbers aspect of it—betrays ignorance of Scripture. *The one is a continuously enduring agency; the other a continually repeated act.*

There is no question, observe, as to whether the benefit depends on the death of Christ. But with some, perhaps, it is a question merely of giving up the " form of sound words " ; with others, the far more solemn one of depreciating the sacrifice of Christ and denying to it an efficacy which even the typical sin-offering possessed for Israel. Christ has died and risen and gone up to God, and now His blood cleanses from all sin. It is not that it avails to accomplish a succession of acts of cleansing for the believer, but that its efficacy remains to cleanse him *continuously*.[1] It is not in order that it may thus cleanse him, that the believer confesses his sin : his only right to the place he holds, even as he confesses, depends on the fact that it does thus cleanse him. It was only in virtue of the place he had through the blood of the lamb that the Israelite could avail himself of the ashes of the red heifer. And our life, our hope, our destiny, depend entirely upon the enduring efficacy of the blood of Christ ; that, whether in bright days of fellowship with God, or in hours of wilderness failure, " the blood cleanseth from all sin " : here it is a question only of the preciousness of that blood, and of the faithfulness and power of Him in Whom we trust.

[1] εἰς τὸ διηνεκές. Heb. x. 14

16

THE PRIESTHOOD OF CHRIST

THE writer of the Hebrews found the truth of the priesthood of the Lord Jesus " hard to be uttered " ; and the reason is obvious, namely, that with the Jew the idea of offering sacrifices for sins was inseparable from priesthood. The fact of the priesthood of Christ thus reacted on the Jewish mind to cast discredit on the sufficiency of the great sacrifice of Calvary ; whereas the teaching of Scripture is unequivocal, that the priesthood of the Son of God is based on eternal redemption accomplished. In a preceding chapter I have dealt with the doctrine of priesthood, but so much confusion of thought exists on this subject, that I may be pardoned perhaps for going into it more closely, even though it should involve some repetition.[1]

[1] At Professor Sanday's Oxford Conference on this subject, the Rev. Mr. Puller of the " Cowley Fathers " was the only member who seemed to grasp the elementary truth that the work of priesthood began after the sacrifice had been killed, and that the priesthood of Christ dates from His ascension. "On earth He would not be a priest at all " (Heb. viii. 4, R.V.).
The R.V. of Heb. v. 1 makes havoc of the truth. It tells us that every high priest is taken from among men, and is appointed to offer sacrifices for sins. The teaching of the verse is correctly given in A.V., that every high priest taken from among men (*i.e.*,

Sin, we as have seen,[1] has a relation both to righteousness and to holiness, but, essentially, it is *lawlessness* : lawlessness and sin are synonymous terms. The answer to the guilt of sin is justification, and to its defilement, sanctification. In virtue of the blood we are both justified and sanctified. But the fact that for the believer guilt is not imputed in no respect changes the essential character of sin. On the contrary, it intensifies the heinousness of it. This, moreover, is the clew to the true character of the Christian life, which is too often lost sight of. Sin against grace is far *more* heinous than sin against law. It is a greater outrage upon God ; and if, as with the Christian, there be a real desire to avoid it, it is a greater proof of weakness.

Here then it is that we learn the power and value of Christ's priestly work. It is not to justify, nor yet to sanctify. These blessings are secured to us in Him in virtue of Calvary. But if we have right thoughts of God and of ourselves, and of the nature of sin, we must know that all the blessings with which grace has crowned us would not avail to maintain us for one hour in the place they give us before God, were it not for what Christ is to us, and for us, in heaven now. In regard to our position under God's moral government we know Him as a Saviour, — " we shall be saved from wrath through Him." [2] In view of fellowship every Aaronic priest) is appointed for that purpose. But our High Priest is the " Son of God " (iv. 14) ; and His priesthood is based upon the Sacrifice which has for ever put away sin, so that now " there is no more offering for sin " (x. 18).

[1] See chap. x.   [2] Rom. v. 9.

in the Father's house we have a Paraclete;[1] and for the sanctuary and the wilderness journey we rejoice to own Him as a great High Priest.

It is with sin then in this its deepest character that priesthood has to do. For the believer, law has no penalties and the glory of the mercy-seat no terrors. The blood has for ever purged his conscience, and there is no question now of guilt; and he stands in indissoluble relationship with God. But it would indeed be strange levity to suppose because of this that sin could fail to cause estrangement. Just in proportion to his knowledge of God, and to his appreciation of the blessings grace has given him, will be his sense of the moral distance between himself and God. The truth that his sin is purged, that he is a child of God, and that he is "accepted in the Beloved," can only serve to make his sin seem blacker. How then can he approach with confidence, and have a *heart* at rest? Here it is that the word comes home to him, "Seeing that we have a great High Priest, Jesus the Son of God, let us come boldly unto the throne of grace that we may obtain mercy."

The answer to the guilt of sin is righteousness, I repeat, and to its defilement, sanctification. And both depend on the blood—the blood shed, and the blood sprinkled. But the answer to the practical estrangement sin produces is reconciliation; and this is the present work of priesthood,

[1] 1 John ii. 1.

" to make reconciliation (or atonement) for the sins of the people." [1]

But this "reconciliation" must not be confounded with the reconciliation treated of in a previous chapter.[2] The latter is a finished work accomplished by the death of Christ, and the sinner enters into the benefit of it by faith; whereas the reconciliation I am now speaking of is the present work of priesthood. They have this in common, however, that both relate to sin in its essential character. Reconciliation for the sinner who believes, is a result of the death of Christ : reconciliation for the believer who sins, depends upon His priesthood. It is akin to the twofold aspect of forgiveness. We *have* the forgiveness of our sins in virtue of redemption ; but yet, in another sense, forgiveness depends upon confession.[3]

And by reason of this it is that, even as sinners, we can come boldly to the throne of grace, confident that we shall find compassion ; not as an encouragement to sin again, but allied with grace to help in time of need. It is because of Him who is sitting

---

[1] Ἱλάσκεσθαι. Every effort has been made to force a meaning on this word, in order to bring in a thought which is wholly opposed to the teaching of the passage. Luke xviii. 13 is the only other place where it occurs ; but it answers in the Septuagint to the Hebrew *to cover*, remove from sight, and, as used of sin, to forgive. Why then suppose it to have a different meaning here ? If what I have said be just, it will be seen how perfectly it expresses the idea intended. It is precisely the truth of 1 John i. 9, but in the Hebrews aspect of it. And note that confession is not to Christ as Priest. Nor does the priest absolve from sin. Here human priestcraft dares to deal with what pertains to God alone.

[2] Chap. x. *ante*. The words for *reconciliation* in the Greek are different.

[3] Compare Eph. i. 7 and Col. i. 14 with 1 John i. 9.

at the right hand of God that the throne of " the Majesty on high " is a throne of grace.

I will not enter on the consideration of Christ's priestly functions in relation to worship, for that lies beyond my subject. But apart from worship, His priestly work, according to the Hebrews, is confined to making reconciliation and intercession. Everything beyond this is mere Judaism or Popery.[1]

Putting aside special teaching, such as the cleansing of the leper, and the consecration of the priests, four of the great types—viz., the Passover, the inauguration of the covenant, and the two principal sin-offerings, of the great day of atonement, and of Numbers xix., may be taken as giving a complete view of what the death of Christ is to us.[2]

As already shown, the two first were not priestly sacrifices. In the third, it was a priest doubtless who led the victim forth, and sprinkled its blood before the tabernacle ; but observe, it was not *Aaron*. The act was typical of the work of Christ, but not of His high-priestly work. A like remark applies to the great day of atonement, when Aaron himself officiated. The ordinance consisted of two distinct parts—first, the sacrifice of sin-offerings, and afterwards of burnt-offerings. Both these were in the highest sense typical of the work of Christ ; but mark the difference in Aaron's position respecting them. For the sin-offering he divested himself of all his high-priestly robes, and put on

[1] Heb. ii. 17 ; iv. 15 ; and vii. 25.

[2] And if we add the burnt-offering, the meat-offering, and the peace-offering (Lev. i., ii., iii.), His work in its highest and Godward aspect, we have the whole in its sevenfold perfectness.

the holy linen garments ; from which we learn that though his action here was typical of what our High-Priest would do for us, this would not be accomplished by Him in His priestly character. The sin-offering concluded in all its parts, Aaron came out in high-priestly splendour, arrayed in his " garments of glory and beauty," and offered the burnt-offerings.[1]

[1] This brings us to the 22nd verse of Ps. xxii., Christ leading the praises of His people (Lev. xvi. 4, 23, 24).

17

ATONEMENT

A WEED has been beautifully described as a plant out of place, and many a heresy is but a perverted truth. The remark is suggested by current theology respecting the Atonement.

The controversy is embarrassed by the ambiguity of the term round which it wages. For the word "atonement" has gradually changed its meaning. "When our translation was made it signified, as innumerable examples prove, reconciliation, or the making up of a foregoing enmity; all its uses in our early literature justifying the etymology now sometimes called into question, that 'atonement' is 'at-one-ment.'"[1] But now the word has come to be accepted as equivalent to "propitiatory sacrifice," and this use is so established that no one may challenge it. Indeed it is occasionally used in that sense in the preceding pages. Here, however, with a view to clearness and accuracy of statement, I will employ it only in its primary meaning, and according to its Biblical usage. In this chapter "atonement" means always and only "at-one-ment."

The real question after all is not as to the use or

[1] Archbishop Trench, *Synonyms.*

meaning of an English word, but as to the doctrinal significance of the language of Scripture. And no one who will be at the pains to study, with the help of a Concordance, the passages in which the Hebrew verb occurs which our translators have commonly rendered " to make atonement," can fail to recognise that under the Mosaic law the at-one-ment was not the sacrifice itself, but a result of sacrifice, depending upon the work of priesthood.[1]

The English reader can judge of this for himself by the use of the word in the book of Leviticus, where it occurs no less than forty-eight times. Its root-meaning may be gleaned from the passage where it first occurs in Scripture. Noah was commanded to *cover* the ark with pitch.[2] From this the transition is easy to its meaning in the second passage where it is used : " I will *appease* him with the present," [3] Jacob said in planning a reconciliation with his brother. To this end he prepared a present ; but the at-one-ment was not the gift itself, neither was it made by preparing the gift ; it was the change to be produced by means of it in Esau's mind toward him. So, also, in Leviticus, the atonement was not the sin-offering, neither was it accomplished by killing the sacrifice ; it depended upon the fulfilment of the prescribed ritual by which persons and things were brought within the benefits of a death already accomplished.

As the New Testament is in great measure written in the language of the Greek version of the Old, we naturally turn to the Epistle to the Hebrews to seek there, in connection with the priesthood of

[1] See Appendix, Note III.   [2] Gen. vi. 14.   [3] Gen. xxxii. 20.

Christ, the word commonly adopted by the LXX. in their rendering of Leviticus. But the significance of the passage where it occurs [1] is obscured or lost by the extraordinary figment that our blessed Lord officiated as a priest at His own death on Calvary. As already shown,[2] the death of Christ was not a priestly sacrifice. The teaching of the New Testament is clear, that it was not till after His ascension that He entered on His priestly office. When, under the old covenant, redemption was accomplished, and Moses, the Mediator of that covenant, had made purification for sins, he went up to God ; and then, and not till then, the high priest was appointed. So also is it with the great antitype.[3] The doctrine of Hebrews is not that Christ's priesthood while on earth was not of the Aaronic order, but that " on earth *He would not be a priest at all.*" [4]

Priesthood has nothing to do with obtaining *redemption*. The 12th chapter of Exodus records the deliverance of Israel both from the doom of Egypt and from the power of Egypt. In the 24th chapter the work was completed by Israel's being brought into covenant relationship with God, and sanctified by the blood with which the covenant was dedicated.[5] Till then, the Divine Majesty forbade the sinner to approach. To touch even the

---

[1] Heb. ii. 17.   [2] Chaps. ix. and xvi. *ante.*
[3] Comp. Ex. xxiv. 8, 15 with Heb. i. 3, and see note 2, p. 123 *ante.*
[4] Heb. viii. 4, R.V. I will not here notice the quibble that on the cross our Lord was *lifted up* from the earth in order that He might be a priest in His death. (See chap. xvi. *ante.*)
[5] Comp. Heb. ix. 19.

base of Sinai was certain and relentless death.[1]
But now that redemption in its fulness was an
accomplished fact, the very men who till then had
been forbidden to " come nigh," were made nigh.
" They saw the God of Israel " ; and in token that
they were at rest in the divine presence, it is added,
" they did eat and drink." [2] Then immediately
follows the command, " Let them make Me a
sanctuary that I may dwell among them." [3]

Without a place of worship there could be no
need for priesthood ; a place of worship was impossible save for a holy people in covenant with
God ; and the covenant was based upon redemption
accomplished. It is at this point also, and that,
too, in connection with the priesthood, that we first
read in Scripture of making atonement for sin. I
have already cited the two earlier passages in which
the Hebrew word occurs ; we next find it here, in
prescribing Aaron's duties.[4] The priest was " appointed for men in things pertaining to God," [5] and
one of his chief functions was " to make an atonement for the children of Israel, for all their sins."

With all this before us, we are in a position to
understand the teaching of Hebrews ii. 17. " In
all things it behoved Him to be made like unto His
brethren, that He might become a merciful and
faithful High Priest in things pertaining to God,
to make atonement for the sins of the people." This
is not redemption for a lost world, but atonement
for the sins of a redeemed people. It is not the
Adamic race that is in question, but " the seed of

[1] Ex. xix. 12, 13. [2] Ex. xxiv. 2, 11. [3] Ex. xxv. 8.
Ex. xxix. 37 , xxx. 10. [5] Heb. v. 1.

Abraham "—the Israel of God (verse 16). The fact is, that in our theology the special truth of atonement has been so confounded with the general truth of redemption, that it is in danger of becoming wholly lost. And prevailing views of sin are so inadequate or false, that Christians are becoming unconscious of the need which the priestly work of Christ alone can satisfy. What Archbishop Trench has written as to Reconciliation, applies here with equal force :—the views now current, views which are leavening all sections of the Church, " rest not on an unprejudiced exegesis, but on a foregone determination to get rid of the reality of God's anger against sin." [1]

And here is the explanation of the seeming paradox of the bloodless sin-offering.[2] The Bible is not a motley compilation of unconnected treatises. The book of Leviticus is based upon the book of Exodus. The offerings it prescribes are for a people who stand in the liberty and joy of redemption. What then if the Israelite, redeemed by the Paschal lamb, and standing within the covenant which secures to him the efficacy of the blood upon the mercy-seat, should be too poor to bring the appointed sacrifice for his trespass ? Divine compassion will reach him in his poverty ; his meat-offering shall be accepted for a sin-offering, and his " sin that he hath sinned shall be forgiven him."

The one offering was as definitely typical of Christ as was the other, and no one may dare to set a limit to the infinite grace of God in His dealings with a sinner who thus turns to Him.

[1] *Synonyms,*   [2] Lev. v 11.

The sinner's sense of sin, and his appreciation of the Sin-bearer, may be so utterly inadequate and poor, that men may set him down as spiritually bankrupt ; and yet if Christ be the ground on which he comes to God, divine grace will reach him. But divine grace is no excuse for human presumption, and this special type only brings into more prominent relief the great truth that, " without shedding of blood there is no remission." As for those who teach a bloodless redemption, the brand of Cain is upon them, for they are murderers of men's souls.

Christ, I repeat, is the antitype of the meat-offering of Leviticus. And there are not many Christs, but only ONE, and He is the Christ of Calvary. But it needs many types and many different images to set forth the immeasurable fulness of all that He is to the sinner. In the preceding pages I have touched upon other aspects of this great truth. Here I will only allude to two. The death of Christ is not merely the sin-offering, but first, and before all, it is the great Redemption sacrifice : " Christ our PASSOVER has been sacrificed." [1] " We have *redemption* through His blood.[2] But redemption, as I have shown, was wholly independent of priesthood, and the *priestly* work of atonement was based upon the sin-offering completed and accepted as complete. The blood carried within the veil was not the completion of the sin-offering, but the memorial of a sin-offering completed.

But what is the blood ? " The life of the flesh is in the blood : and I have given it to you upon

[1] 1 Cor. v. 7.   [2] Eph. i. 7.

the altar to make an atonement for your souls." [1]
From this it is argued that the blood represents not
death but life. If this meant merely that all our
blessings depend upon a living Christ, the doctrine
would be right, though wrongly expressed, and
based on a wrong text. That Christ made propitiation for our sins is the language of theology :
that Christ IS the propitiation for our sins is the
teaching of Scripture.[2] Our Saviour is not a dead
Christ upon a cross, but a living Christ upon the
throne. But His right and title to be a Saviour
depends upon the cross. He " *died* for our sins,
according to the Scriptures, and was buried and
rose again the third day, according to the Scriptures." Such is " the Gospel by which we are
saved." [3] There is not a word about His " offering
Himself to the Father " in resurrection.

But did not Christ enter heaven with His own
blood ? And, if blood be life, must not this mean
that He entered there in virtue of the life which He
carried through death, and presented in resurrection as an offering to God ?

This theory is based upon a superficial study of
the types, and it is in a fuller knowledge of the
types that the refutation of it will be found. Some
there are who need to be reminded that when
Scripture speaks of Christ's entering heaven with
His own blood, the language is purely figurative.
But the figure is typical, not fanciful. And every
figure has a reality of which it is but the shadow ;
every type has its antitype. It is forgotten, moreover, that Aaron's entering within the veil is not

[1] Lev. xvii. 11.   [2] I John ii. 2.   [3] I Cor. xv. 1-4.

the only type of the ascension ; and it is to a wholly different type that prominence is given in the 9th chapter of Hebrews. The 13th verse brackets together the two principal sin-offerings of Leviticus xvi. and Numbers xix. ; but in the 12th verse the reference is not to the sin-offering at all, but to the great sacrifice of Exodus xxiv. which completed their redemption. " Neither by the blood of *goats and calves* [compare verse 19], but by His own blood He entered in once for all into the holy place [not, " to make atonement," but] having obtained eternal *redemption*." It is not the Priest going in to finish an unfinished work, but the Mediator going in on the ground of a work finished and complete.

Aaron passing within the veil was the correlative of Moses going up into the mount. This latter type, which is the key-note to the Epistle to the Hebrews (see chapter i. 3), is, as above noticed, taken up in the 12th verse and resumed in the passage beginning at the 19th verse. But the two types are so blended together throughout that the superficial reader entirely fails to notice the emphatic reference to the Mediator. In the one, Moses entered the divine presence by the blood of the redemption sacrifices ; in the other, Aaron entered the divine presence by the blood of the sin-offering. Whatever the blood means in the one case it means also in the other ; and by its meaning in these grouped and blended types, we must interpret the language when thus applied to Christ. But the teaching of Hebrews is clear and unequivocal, that the blood of the Covenant represented *death*.[1]

[1] Heb. ix. 11-20.

Moses, therefore, ascended the Mount and stood in the presence of the thrice holy God, not on the ground of life, but on the ground of a death accomplished.[1]

If Christ has entered heaven on the ground of life, He is there on a ground which hopelessly excludes a creature who is under the death-sentence pronounced on sin. Therefore it is that such emphasis rests upon the blood. The cross is His title to the throne, and this title He can share with sinners who by faith become one with Him in the death He died to sin.

" The life of the flesh is in the blood," that is, in " the warm and living blood " which animates it. Therefore it is that, when the organism is destroyed by the pouring out of that which energised it, the blood, now cold and still, represents life laid down and lost. In a word, it represents *death*. Take yet another type. When the death-sentence fell upon " all the firstborn in the land of Egypt," the Israelite escaped because the appointed sacrifice had been slain, and the blood was on the lintel and the door-posts of his home. Was it the victim's "warm and living blood " that turned away the angel of death ? Was it (to borrow a phrase from this heresy) the " *living* life " of the Paschal lamb ? The question needs only to be clothed in words in order to make the answer clear The destroying angel was turned aside from the blood-stained house because the judgment had already fallen there.

[1] And this is precisely the thought implied in the διά of the 12th verse and the ἐν of the 25th. There is a great deal of theology in prepositions, and if the doctrine were what these teachers tell us, a language so rich in prepositions as the Greek would give clear expression to it.

Death was already past, and the sprinkled blood was the memorial of that death.

And this too was the significance of the sprinkled blood within the veil, which had continuing efficacy to cleanse from sin. How can any one picture to himself those foul, black stains upon the golden mercy-seat, and yet imagine that they represented life in its activities, presented in joyful service to God! If such were the teaching, is it possible to conceive any symbolism more inapt? Imagine a bereaved mother or wife bedaubing her home with the blood of a dead child or husband in order to keep fresh in her heart the great fact and truth of *life!*

The sight of a room thus stained will not easily fade from my memory. It was the scene of the last and most fiendish of the crimes known as the "Whitechapel murders" in London. Blood was on the furniture, blood was on the floor, blood was on the walls, blood was everywhere. Did this speak to me of life? Yes, but of life gone, of life destroyed, and, therefore, of that which is the very antithesis of life. Every blood-stain in that horrid room spoke of *death*.

And here I ask the question, If God intended to teach the truth that the sinner could approach Him only on the ground of death, could divine wisdom find a fitter symbol than that the priest should carry with him into His presence the blood of the vicarious sacrifice? If, on the other hand, any one seeks thus to enforce the doctrine which these teachers would connect with it, we may well exclaim, Could perverted ingenuity suggest an imagery more incongruous and false! To teach that poured-out, putrefying blood represents not death but life, is not only a departure from the truth of Scripture, but an outrage upon the commonest instincts of mankind.

18

THE GODHOOD OF GOD

It is matter for reflection whether the want of such a word as " Godhood " has not helped to let the thought it signifies die out

Whether men believe it or not, Jehovah is GOD This is a fact absolute and certain. But is He *my* God ? The Psalmist could say, " O God, Thou art *my* God ! " Does this mean no more than that He was God ? He was the God of Israel ; but if any one imagines that He was the God of Pharaoh, or of the Philistines, or of the kings of Canaan, he must have strange ideas of what it is to have a God Because He was the God of Israel, He destroyed the power of Pharaoh in order to deliver them. If the sea barred their way, He made a highway through it If they hungered, the heaven rained bread ; if they thirsted, the rock gave forth water in the midst of the desert. And the tribes of the wilderness and the nations of the land, as they heard that battle-shout from the puny armies of Israel, " The Lord of Hosts is with us, the God of Jacob is our refuge." could have taught the Christians of to-day what it means to have Jehovah for our God. God was not *their* God, but He was the God of Israel.

And can any thoughtful man look abroad upon

the world, and imagine for a moment that God is a God to creation now ? " The whole creation *groans*." The children of Israel groaned in Egyptian bondage, but when, their deliverance complete, they stood around their glorious king in their glorious city, it was no longer a groan that rose to heaven, but shouts of praise and the worship of full hearts. And when God becomes once again a God to all His creatures, their groans will no more be heard. The creation shall then be " delivered from the bondage of corruption into the glorious liberty of the children of God." [1] Then " shall the Lord rejoice in His works," and from His opened hand the desire of *every living thing* shall be satisfied.[2]

Men delight to speak of the Fatherhood of God,[3] because they think it gives them claims on Him. And doubtless they who are indeed His children have real claims upon God in virtue of the tie. Though even here there is need to remember that a relationship cannot be wholly on one side : " *If I am a Father*, where is mine honour ? " [4] God may well demand. But what is usually meant by the Fatherhood of God is really His *Godhood*. And if God was the God of Israel there were *mutual* obligations involved in the relationship. And so it must ever be. But men speak as though the fact of their being His creatures gave them claims on God, while they utterly forget that sin is a repudiation of His claims on them—a denial of the very relationship on which they insist so strongly when their own interests are concerned.

[1] Rom. viii 21. [2] Ps. civ. 31 and cxlv. 16.
[3] See Appendix. Note IV. [4] Mal. i. 6.

Moreover, as we have seen,[1] by the rejection of Christ man forfeits every claim of every kind on God ; while, in the gospel, the grace of God presents Christ as the fulfilment of every blessing which a loving God can bestow. God has far different thoughts toward the " Canaanite " and the " Philistine " of to-day than were expressed by the sword of Israel. It is not that the human heart is changed, still less the heart of God ; but that the work of Christ has enabled God to assume a new attitude toward men. " In Christ He was reconciling the world unto Himself " ; " The God of our Lord Jesus Christ " can now become a God to all, because, I repeat once more, RECONCILIATION is accomplished.[2]

But if men reject Christ, and refuse the reconciliation, how can there possibly be mercy for them ? In past dispensations man's sin and failure have always drawn out some better thing from God's great goodness and wisdom and power ; but, now, the climax has been reached. His best gift has been given ; His masterwork has been achieved ; heaven is flung wide open, and sinful men are called to fellowship with Christ in His glory. Divine love and grace are now exhausted, and the only possible alternative and sequel is VENGEANCE. If men insist on defying God and maintaining the place of

[1] See chap. ii. *ante.*

[2] And this, I venture to believe, is the *peace-offering* aspect of the work of Christ—the fulfilment of the third great type which, with the burnt-offering and the meat-offering, represents the work of Christ in its Godward aspect. The burnt-offering is His complete surrender of Himself to God ; the meat-offering the perfectness of the Man who did so dedicate Himself ; and the peace-offering, the results to Godward of that sacrifice.

adversaries, there can be nothing for them but " judgment and fiery indignation which shall devour *the adversaries*."

By Godhood then I mean the relationship existing between God and His creatures in virtue of His Godhead. That relationship was outraged and set aside by sin, and even the lower creation shared the blight which fell upon our world because of it. But " by the blood of the cross " God has reconciled all things to Himself. The enjoyment of this benefit [1] is postponed for " the creation " until the " manifestation of the sons of God," [2] and it will be lost for ever by impenitent men. But the reconciliation is a fact and a truth for the believer, here and now, and he has access to it, and ought to be in the joy of it.

But the Godhood of God toward the believer is true only to *faith*. The Christian's God is " the God of our Lord Jesus Christ," [3] for even such an one as *He* had a God ; and yet the Lord Jesus knew what it was to be in want. The universe was His creature, and by a word He could make bread for starving thousands, or crown the provision for a feast with richest wine ; but when it was Himself who hungered or was athirst, He looked up and trusted in His God. He had a God, and yet He had not where to lay His head.

And as it was with the Leader of Faith, so has it been with the sons of Faith in every age. In the 11th chapter of Hebrews we read of some " who through faith subdued kingdoms, wrought righteousness, obtained promises, stopped the mouths of

[1] χάρισμα, Rom. v. 15.   [2] Rom. viii. 19.   [3] Eph. i 17.

lions, quenched the violence of fire, escaped the edge of the sword, out of weakness were made strong, waxed valiant in fight, turned to flight the armies of the aliens." But we read of others who, none the less through faith, " were tortured, *not accepting deliverance*," and of others again who " had trial of cruel mockings and scourgings, yea, moreover, of bonds and imprisonment. They were stoned, they were sawn asunder, were tempted, were slain with the sword ; they wandered about in sheepskins and goatskins, being destitute, afflicted, tormented." And to these it is that the divine epitaph belongs, " Of whom the world was not worthy."

The faith that bears and suffers, is greater than the faith that triumphs. How many there are who, through ignorance of this mystery of faith, have made shipwreck of their hopes, and are sunk under trial and disappointment. Faith must be prepared for a refusal. Faith trusts for safety, but never fails when perils come. Faith looks for food and shelter, but never falters when " hunger, and thirst, and cold, and nakedness " become its portion. The faith that cries with the Psalmist, " At *midnight* I will rise to give thanks unto Thee," is truer and greater than the faith that could bid the sun stand still upon Gibeon ; and the sufferings of Paul denote a higher faith than the mightiest acts of Elijah. " In deaths oft. Of the Jews five times received I forty stripes save one. Thrice was I beaten with rods ; once was I stoned ; thrice I suffered shipwreck ; a night and a day I have been in the deep. . . . In weariness and painfulness, in watchings often, in hunger and thirst, in fastings often, in cold and nakedness."

" A night and a day have I been in the deep ! " Paul—the beloved child and saint of God, the faithful and honoured servant, the chosen vessel to bear His name before the world, the foremost of the apostles—clinging to some frail plank upon the wild lone sea, hour after hour for a whole sun's round ; in hunger, and thirst, and cold ; the sport of every wave ; lost to earth, and seemingly unknown to heaven ; and yet he had a God who could have delivered him by a word ! And though deliverance came not, he kept his heart and eye fixed upon unseen realities, and reckoned the present sufferings unworthy to be compared with the coming glory.

Even in the midst of sorrow and trial, happiness is the Christian's lot. Happiness : not the flippant gaiety of a careless heart (for if, even in the world, such happiness is contemptible—the uncoveted monopoly of fools—how utterly unworthy is it of those who have been called to fellowship with the sufferings of Christ !) but happiness in the truer and deeper sense in which alone the Scripture speaks of it.[1] The highest type of existence is not the butterfly, but " The Man of Sorrows "—He of the marred visage and the melted heart.

Such then is the Christian's happiness. Through all circumstances, and in spite of them, he is a prosperous man, a *blessed* man. He may indeed

[1] There is no word for *happy* in the Bible, save in its good old meaning of fortunate, or *blessed*. (Compare, *e.g.*, Matt. v. 10, 11 with 1 Pet. iii. 14, iv. 14.)

have care and trial and sorrow ; but his is the God who, while He could leave His child to be a solitary and outcast wanderer, with no pillow but a stone, and no companion but a staff, could yet turn that stone into a memorial pillar of thanksgiving and praise, and make that loneliness the very gate of heaven ! "*Happy* is he that has the God of Jacob for his help ! " " Happy the people whose God is Jehovah ! " [1]

" SAFE "

Safe in Jehovah's keeping,
  Led by His glorious arm,
God is Himself my refuge,
  A present help from harm.
Fears may at times distress me,
  Griefs may my soul annoy ;
God is my strength and portion,
  God my exceeding joy.

Safe in Jehovah's keeping,
  Safe in temptation's hour,
Safe in the midst of perils,
  Kept by Almighty power.
Safe when the tempest rages,
  Safe though the night be long ;
E'en when my sky is darkest,
  God is my strength and song.

Sure is Jehovah's promise,
  Nought can my hope assail ;
Here is my soul's sure anchor,
  Entered within the veil.
Blest in His love eternal,
  What can I want beside !
Safe through the blood that cleanseth
  Safe in the Christ that died.

---

[1] Ps. cxliv. 15, and cxlvi. 5.

APPENDICES

Note 1 (page 50)

Note 1 (page 50)

MIRACLES

THE subject of miracles, and of " evidences " in general, is too large to treat of here ; but yet the reference I have made to them compels me to add a few remarks.

1st. The mere fact of miracles is no proof of divine intervention. A miracle is such an interference with the course of nature as is beyond our own power. Any creature, therefore, entirely superior to us can perform what we deem a miracle. The miracles worked by Satan in the temptation of our Lord (Luke iv. 5) are far more wonderful (I do not say " greater ") than all the miracles of all the apostles combined ; and Scripture testifies that the devil will again exert miraculous power on earth.

2nd. Miracles are never appealed to in Scripture as " an evidence," save in connection with a preceding revelation to which they are referred. The gospel of Christ was not " the beginning of the oracles of God " ; it was another chapter in a long-continued revelation. But it had a two-fold aspect. He came to a people whose every hope for earth and heaven centred in a Messiah promised to their fathers, and He came, moreover, to a world that was ruined and lost. His mission, therefore, had a twofold character and purpose. He was the Messiah to the Jew ; He was the bread of God to give life to the world. It was with the former that the miracles had specially to do   The knowledge of His higher mission and character was not an inference from miracles.   It was the subject of a special revelation to John the Baptist, and through him to those who afterwards became the first disciples of the Lord (John i. 33–37).   These all belonged to the little company spoken of in Luke ii. 38 as waiting for the redemption of Israel.   They followed Him because they were already God's people, and yet even these needed a word from God to enable them to know Him.

3rd. If this be so, we shall expect to find that it was to Jews that the testimony was based on miracles, and that when the kingdom gospel, or special national testimony, ceased, miracles became of secondary importance.   Both these points are plain upon the face of Scripture.   As soon as the Sanhedrim decreed the destruction of Christ, He sought to keep His miracles secret (Matt. xii. 14–16).   He could not be face to face with need and refuse to meet it, but He no longer wished the fame of His power to go forth. And when, after His final rejection, the gospel became a purely spiritual testimony, miracles were never appealed to in confirmation of it.   The national testimony which the apostles had been sent forth to render at the first was based on miracles (Matt. x. 7, 8).   The gospel of Pentecost was a living power, independent of all extrinsic proof ; it was itself the means of the conversion of 3000 souls (Acts ii. 41).

" To the Jew first," is characteristic of the Acts, and of the transitional period the book embraces.   After the conversion of Cornelius, the public testimony was no longer confined to the Jew, but the Jew retained the right to priority in the offer of grace (see *ex. gr.* Acts xiii. 46).   The miracles therefore continued, though without their former prominence.   And when Paul went forth preaching to Gentiles, miracles seem to have been divorced from his testimony.   His miracle at Lystra was in response to the faith of the man who was the subject of it (Acts xiv. 9) ;

and the effect it had upon those who witnessed it was that, they owned the apostles as gods, as was natural with heathens, and prepared to sacrifice to them. So was it also at Melita (Acts xxviii. 6).

That miraculous power existed in Gentile Churches the 12th chapter of 1st Corinthians establishes; but the question is, Did the gospel which produced those Churches appeal to miracles to confirm it? Can any one read the first four chapters of that very Epistle, and retain a doubt as to the answer?

The great question here involved resolves itself, sooner or later, into this: When God speaks to man's heart through the gospel, does He speak in such wise that the word carries with it the certainty that it is from Him? To say that God cannot do this is to deny that He is supreme; and to deny a Supreme Being is sheer Atheism. To say that He does not is to remove the truth of revelation out of the region of certainty altogether. For the genuineness of miracles must, of course, depend on evidence; and if, as Paley declares, the reality of a revelation must be proved by miracles, it is only by weighing evidences that we can determine what is revealed; and that form of proof can never, in such matters, reach higher than probability. Indeed, no accurate or astute thinker has ever claimed more for it. The degree of conviction thus attainable is, doubtless, an overwhelming condemnation of the infidel, but it is a poor substitute for the faith of the Christian.

According to Paley, the value of the Christian revelation is determined by the miracles. According to Scripture, the value of the miracles was determined by the revelation. It was not that miracles were wrought, but that the miracles of the ministry were precisely what Isaiah prophesied the Messiah would accomplish.

The whole system is false, and must drive simple-minded folk to Rome; for the many are quite incapable of reasoning out Christianity from evidences, and, if that be our only foundation, they must trust the Church. With what a sense of relief we turn to a word like this, " I thank Thee, O Father, Lord of heaven and earth, because Thou hast hid these things from the wise and prudent, and hast revealed them unto babes."

I have dealt with this subject in *The Silence of God*, Chapters III., IV., and V.

Note 2 (page 169)

ἁγιάζω.

Matt. vi. 9.—" *Hallowed* be Thy name " (and Luke xi. 2).

Matt. xxiii. 17, 19.—The temple that *sanctifieth* the gold : the altar that *sanctifieth* the gift.

John x. 36.—Say ye of Him whom the Father hath *sanctified*.

John xvii. 17, 19.—*Sanctify* them through Thy truth. For their sakes I *sanctify* myself, that they also might be *sanctified* through the truth.

Acts xx. 32.—Inheritance among all them that are *sanctified* (and xxvi. 18).

Rom. xv. 16.—That the offering up of the Gentiles might be acceptable, being *sanctified* by the Holy Ghost.

1 Cor. i. 2.—*Sanctified* in Christ Jesus.

1 Cor. vi. 11.—But ye are *sanctified* . . . by the Spirit of our God.

1 Cor. vii. 14.—The unbelieving husband is *sanctified* by the wife, and the unbelieving wife is *sanctified* by the husband.

Eph. v. 26.—That He might *sanctify* it (the Church).

1 Thess. v. 23.—God of peace *sanctify* you wholly.

1 Tim. iv. 5.—(Every creature) is *sanctified* by the Word of God and prayer.

2 Tim. ii. 21.—A vessel *sanctified* and meet for the Master's use.

Heb. ii. 11.—He that *sanctifieth* and they who are *sanctified*.

Heb. ix. 13.—If blood . . . *sanctifieth* to the purifying of the flesh.

Heb. x. 10.—By which will we are *sanctified*.

Heb. x. 14.—Hath perfected them that are *sanctified*.

Heb. x. 29.—Blood . . . wherewith he was *sanctified*.

Heb. xiii. 12.—That He might *sanctify* the people.

1 Pet. iii. 15.—*Sanctify* in your hearts Christ as Lord (R.V.).

Jude 1.—To them that are *sanctified* by God the Father (the Revised reading is *beloved* in God the Father).

Rev. xxii. 11.—Let him be holy still (literally, let him be *sanctified* still).

ἁγιασμός.

Rom. vi. 19.—Yield your members servants to righteousness unto *holiness*.

Rom. vi. 22.—Ye have your fruit unto *holiness*.

1 Cor. i. 30.—Christ is made unto us . . . *sanctification*.

1 Thess. iv. 3.—This is the will of God, even your *sanctification*, that ye should abstain from fornication.

1 Thess. iv. 4.—Possess his vessel in *sanctification*.

1 Thess. iv. 7.—God hath not called us to uncleanness, but to *holiness*.

2 Thess. ii. 13.—Salvation through *sanctification* of the Spirit and belief of the truth.

1 Tim. ii. 15.—Saved in childbearing if they continue in *holiness*.

Heb. xii. 14.—Follow . . . *holiness*, without which no man shall see the Lord.

1 Pet. i. 2.—Elect . . . through *sanctification* of the Spirit unto, etc.

Note 3 (page 186)

Caphar and ἱλάσκομαι.

In the Septuagint, ἐξιλάσκομαι is usually the equivalent of the Hebrew *Caphar*. This word (ἱλάσκομαι) occurs but twice in the New Testament—viz., Luke xviii. 13, and Hebrews ii. 17. Of the latter I have spoken. As regards the publican's prayer, compare Deut. xxi. 8, and passages like 2 Chron. xxx. 18, where the word occurs in the LXX.

The allied substantives, ἱλαστήριον and ἱλασμός, occur twice, and only twice ; the former in Rom. iii. 25 (propitiation), and Heb. ix. 5 (mercy-seat) ; the latter in 1 John ii. 2, and iv. 10. The mercy-seat or " propitiatory " was the meeting-place between God and the accepted sinner, and it was this in virtue of the blood. So Christ has been " set forth to be a propitiatory," but the Word emphatically adds " *through faith in His* blood." He is the propitiatory where God can meet the sinner, because He is Himself the propitiation, and He is the propitiation in virtue of His death for sin.

The following is a list of the passages where the Hebrew word *Caphar* is used. The Authorised Version rendering is given where it is translated otherwise than by *make atonement*. (The references are to the English Bible, not the Hebrew.)

Gen. vi. 14 (*pitch*) ; xxxii. 20 (*appease*).

Ex. xxix. 33, 36, 37 ; xxx. 10 (twice), 15, 16 ; xxxii. 30.

Lev. i. 4 ; iv. 20, 26, 31, 35 ; v. 6, 10, 13, 16, 18 ; vi. 7, 30 (*reconcile*) ; vii. 7 ; viii. 15 (*make reconciliation*), 34 ; ix. 7 (twice) ; x. 17 ; xii. 7, 8 ; xiv. 18, 19, 20, 21, 29, 31, 53 ; xv. 15, 30 ; xvi. 6, 10, 11, 16, 17 (twice), 18, 20 (*reconciling*), 24, 27, 30, 32, 33 (thrice), 34 ; xvii. 11 (twice) ; xix. 22 ; xxiii. 28.

Num. v. 8 ; vi. 11 ; viii. 12, 19, 21 ; xv. 25, 28 (twice) ; xvi. 46, 47 ; xxv. 13 ; xxviii. 22, 30 ; xxix. 5 ; xxxi. 50 ; xxxv. 33 (*cleansed*).

Deut. xxi. 8 (twice ; *Be merciful* and *shall be forgiven*) ; xxxii.
43 (*will be merciful*).
1 Sam. iii. 14 (*be purged*).
2 Sam. xxi. 3.
1 Chron. vi. 49.
2 Chron. xxix. 24 ; xxx. 18 (*pardon*).
Neh. x. 33.
Ps. lxv. 3 (*purge away*) ; lxxviii. 38 (*forgave*) ; lxxix. 9
(*purge away*).
Prov. xvi. 6 (*is purged*), 14 (*pacify*).
Isa. vi. 7 (*purged*) ; xxii. 14 (*purged*) ; xxvii. 9 (*purged*) ;
xxviii. 18 (*be disannulled*) ; xlvii. 11 (*put it off*).
Jer. xviii. 23 (*forgive*).
Ezek. xvi. 63 (*am pacified*) ; xliii. 20 (*purge*), 26 (*purge*) ;
xlv. 15 and 17 (*make reconciliation*) ; xlv. 20 (*reconcile*).
Dan. ix. 24 (*make reconciliation*).

The substantive *kippûr* occurs in the following passages :

Ex. xxix. 36 ; xxx. 10, 16.
Lev. xxiii. 27, 28 ; xxv. 9.
Num. v. 8 ; xxix. 11.

Note 4 (page 197)

THE FATHERHOOD OF GOD

The figment of the universal Fatherhood of God is one of
the most popular of heresies. With those who hold that
man is the product of evolution the claim is obviously
fanciful. Nor is it much better in the case of those who

accept the truth of Scripture. For we are not the children of Adam as he came from the hand of God, but the remote descendants of the sinful and fallen outcast of Eden. And were it not that in the sphere of religion people seem to take leave not only of their Bibles but of their brains, they would recognise that this cannot constitute us children of God in the Scriptural sense.

True it is that in order to expose the error and folly of thinking " that the Godhead is like unto gold or silver or stone, graven by art and man's device," the Apostle Paul when addressing a heathen audience adopted the words of a heathen poet, " For we are also His offspring " (Acts xvii. 28, 29). But no doctrine of sonship can be based on this. The word here used (*genos*) is one of wide significance ; and the argument founded upon it would be equally valid if the lower creation were intended.

Heb. ii. 14 is also appealed to in support of this figment. But the words of verse 16 are explicit :—" He taketh hold of the seed of Abraham." " We must not here understand *mankind*, as some have done," is Dean Alford's obvious comment. The " children " of verse 14 are not the seed of Adam but " *the seed of Abraham* " ; that is, the children of faith. We become children of God, not by descent from Adam, but by faith in Christ. The teaching of Scripture here is definite and clear : " As many as received Him, to them gave He the right to become children of God, even to them that believe in His name, *which were born . . . of God* " (John i. 12, 13). This is the test. The relationship depends on birth. " Except a man be born again he cannot see the kingdom of God " (John iii. 3). Most certain it is, therefore, that he cannot be a child of God. Still more terribly explicit were the Lord's words to the religious leaders who rejected Him. Said He : " Ye are of your father the devil, and the lusts of your father it is your will to do " (John viii. 44). This heresy teaches that we are *by nature* children of God : the Scripture declares that we are " *by nature* children of wrath " (Eph. ii. 3).

INDEX

Aaron, priesthood of, 124, 129 *n.*, 183.
Alford, Dean, quoted, 108 *n.*, 111 *n.*, 124 *n.*, 137 *n.*, 148 *n.*, 166, 210.
Ascension, types of the, 191, 192.
Atonement, 185–195.

Blood, typical meaning of, 173, 190–195 (and see Chaps. IX. and XIII.)
  ,,   washing in, 175 *n.*
Bloodless sin-offering, the, 189.
Bloomfield, quoted, 108 *n.*, 109 *n.*
Bonar, Horatius, quoted, 69–70 *n.*
Butler, Bishop, quoted, 28, 45 *n.*, 51, 165.

"Christian," origin of name, 130 *n.*
Cleansing by blood, 173–178.
  ,,   by water, 127, 175 *n.*
Confession of sin, 128, 177.
Conversion, 63.
Cornelius, 41 *n.*
Creation, reconciliation for the, 145,149.
  ,,   the new, 114–115, 133, 172.
Cross, the, 24–37.
  ,,   the offence of, 27–29.

Deacons, 7 *n.*
Dispensational truth, 9, 104 *n.*

Election, 75–86.
Evil, origin of, 105 *n.*, 143–144.

Faith, 38–55, 153–158.
  ,,   of a record, 39–43.
  ,,   in a person, 46.
  ,,   as trust, 39, 154.
  ,,   with the heart, 44.
  ,,   *in* or *on* Christ, 155–156.
  ,,   supernatural, 33.
  ,,   of the Christian life, 199–201.
Fatherhood of God, 150, 197, 210.

Gnostic philosophy, 147–148.
Godhood of God, 144, 196–202.
Gospel, greatness of the, 2.
  ,,   incredibility of the, 33, 166.
  ,,   Scriptural statement of the, 43, 79, 88–96.
  ,,   true for all, 86, 94.
Grace, 9–20, 85, 101, 116.
Greek words—
    ἁγιάζειν, 168, 206.
    ἁγιασμός, 133 *n.*, 168, 170, 207
    ἁγιότης, 171.
    ἁγιωσύνη, 171.
    ἀντί, 95 *n.*
    διάκονος, διακονία, 8 *n.*
    δικαίωμα, 166.
    δικαίωσις, 166.
    ἱλάσκομαι, 182 *n.*, 208.
    ἱλαστήριον, 208.
    ἱλασμός, 208.
    καθαρίζειν, 173 *n.*
    καταλλαγή, 140 *n.*
    λουτρόν, 169 *n.*
    μεταμέλομαι, 58 *n.*
    μετάνοια, 58 *n.*, 59.
    νόμος, 108 *n.*
    ὁσιότης, 133 *n.*, 171.
    πάρεσις, 111 *n.*
    πιστεύειν εἰς, π. ἐπί, 156 *n.*
    σωτήριος, 80 *n.*, 116 *n.*
    ὑπέρ, 95 *n.*
    χάρισμα, 141 *n.*
Green, S. G., quoted, 108 *n.*

Happy, Happiness, 201.
Heathen, fate of the, 11
Hebrews, Epistle to the, 118, 122, 129 *n.*, 179, 186.
Holiness and sanctification, 168.
Holy Spirit (*see* Spirit).

James, Epistle of, 159, 160.
Judgment, the, 10, 17, 18 *n.*, 145, 147

Justification by blood, 101, 163.
,, by faith, 102, 153.
,, by grace, 101 ff.
,, by works, 159.

Kant's philosophy, 77, 78, 80 n.

Law, the, 107 ff., 164.
Leper, the cleansing of the, 32 n., 91, 92, 93.

Marriage Supper, parable of the, 113 n.
Ministry, fitness for the, 4-7.
Miracles, evidential value of, 49-52, 203.

New birth, the, 64, 66 n.
Nicodemus, 65, 66, 67.

Offerings, the typical offerings, 32, 120, 175 ff., 189-192.
,, burnt-offering, 32 n., 120, 183 n., 198 n.
,, cleansing of the leper, 32 n., 91.
,, Day of Atonement, 99 n., 174-177, 183, 191, 192.
,, Dedication of the Covenant, 120, 187, 192.
,, meat-offering, 189, 198 n.
,, Passover, 89, 90, 119, 174.
,, peace-offering, 198 n.
,, sin-offerings (ordinary), 126, 132 n., 176, 189.
,, "water of purification," 66 n., 127, 129, 132 n., 177.

Paley on miracles, 205.
Paul, the ministry of, 4-7, 28-30, 200.
Poetry—
"The Night of the Betrayal," 20.
"The Prodigal's Return," 71.
"Safe," 202.

Prayer, 69, 81-82.
Priesthood, 119, 123-125, 128, 181, 190.
,, of Christ, 125, 128-129, 179-184, 187.
Probation of man closed, 106-107.
Punishment, eternal, 150, 198.

Reconciliation, 136 ff, 198-199.
,, Priestly, 182.
Redemption, twofold aspect of, 88-89.
Repentance, 56 ff.
,, twofold bearing of, 61.
Righteousness, Chaps. VIII., XI., XII. and XIII. (and see Justification).
,, human, 107.
Roman military triumphs, 3, 19.
Romans, thesis of the Epistle to the, 103, 136.

"Safe," 202.
Saints, meaning and use of the word, 130.
Sanctification, Chaps. IX. and XIV.
,, absolute, 121-122, 134, 169, 170.
,, continuous, 130-131, 134, 170.
,, progressive, 131, 171.
,, intrinsic, 133, 168.
Sanday, Prof., 179 n.
Sin, nature of, 107 n., 143, 144, 181.
Spirit, work of the Holy, 45 n., 56 ff.
Substitution, 87 ff.

Trench, Archbishop, 185, 189.

Washing with blood, 175 n.
,, with water, 127-128, 175 n.
Water, typical meaning of, 66 n. (and see Cleansing).
Whitechapel murders, 194.
Works, justification by, 159 ff.

SCRIPTURE INDEX

Matt. xi. 2, 3, p. 50.
    xxii. 11–13, p. 113 *n*.

Luke iv. 16–20, p. 18 *n*.
    xvi. 16, p. 104 *n*.

John i. 11, p. 13 *n*.
    ii. 23, 24, p. 50.
    iii. 5, p. 66 *n*.
    vi. 28–29, p. 12.
    xii. 31, p. 14.
    xvi. 8–11, pp. 68, 108.

Acts xiii. 46, p. 165.
    xiv. 8–18, p. 10.
    xvii. 22–31, p. 11.
    xix. 4, p. 62.

Rom. i. 4, p. 171.
    i. 17, p. 103.
    i. 20, p. 11.
    ii. 6–11, p. 10.
    iii. 8, p. 104 *n*.
    ,, 20, p. 108.
    ,, 21, p. 109.
    ,, 24, p. 101.
    ,, 25, p. 111.
    v. 1, p. 137.
    ,, 9, pp. 101, 163.
    ,, 10, p. 141 *n*.
    ,, 11, p. 140.
    ,, 12–21, pp. 19, 141, 142.
    ,, 18, 19, p. 166.
    vi. 1–4, p. 96.
    viii. 4, p. 166 *n*.
    ,, 19–22, pp. 145, 199.
    x. 5–10, p. 43.
    ,, 17, pp. 38, 54.

1 Cor. i. 18, p. 24.
    ,, 30, pp. 115, 172.
    vi. 11, p. 170.
    xv. 24–28, pp. 151, 152.
    ,, 41, p. 28 *n*.

2 Cor. ii. 14–16, pp. 4, 31.
    ,, 17, p. 27.
    iii. 5–11, pp. 4, 5.

2 Cor. v. 19–21, pp. 96 *n*., 141.
    vii. 1, pp. 129–131.
    xii. 9, 10, p. 6.

Gal. ii. 21, p. 110.
    v. 2, p. 29.
    ,, 11, pp. 25, 30.
    vi. 15, p. 114.

Eph. ii. 8 pp. 54 *n*., 80.
    iv. 24, pp. 133 *n*., 171.
    v. 26, p. 169.

Col. i. 15–20 pp. 148, 149.
    ,, 23, p. 145.
    ii. 15, p. 19.

1 Thess. v. 23, p. 169.

1 Tim. i. 11, p. 9.
    iii. 8–13, p. 7 *n*.

Tit. ii. 11, pp. 80, 116.

Heb. i. 3, p. 123.
    ii. 17, pp. 181, 187, 188.
    iv. 15, p. 124 *n*.
    v. 1, p. 179 *n*.
    vii. 12, p. 125.
    viii. 4, pp. 179 *n*., 187.
    ix. 12, 13, p. 191.
    x. 10, p. 120.

James ii. 18–24, pp. 159–162.

1 Pet. i. 1, p. 120 *n*.
    i. 2, pp. 170, 173.

2 Pet. i. 20, p. 59.

1 John i. 7–10, pp. 128 *n*., 173–178.
    iii. 4, pp. 107, 143.
    v. 1, 5, p. 33.
    ,, 1–11, p. 42.

Rev. i. 5, p. 175 *n*.
    vii. 14, p. 176 *n*.
    xxii. 14, p. 176 *n*.